# Ladybugs

## *Teacher's Guide*

### Preschool — 1

### Skills
Observing, Identifying, Creative and Logical Thinking,
Communicating, Comparing, Matching, Role Playing

### Concepts
Ladybugs (Body Structure, Life Cycle, Defenses), Symmetry,
Predator/Prey, Environmental Role of Ladybugs

### Themes
Systems & Interactions, Patterns of Change, Models & Simulations,
Evolution, Scale, Structure, Diversity & Unity

### Math Strands
Geometry (Symmetry), Pattern,
Number, Measurement, Logic

by
## Jean C. Echols

**LHS GEMS**

**GEMS**
Great Explorations in Math and Science
Lawrence Hall of Science
University of California at Berkeley

Lawrence Hall of Science
University of California
Berkeley, CA 94720

Chairman: Glenn T. Seaborg
Director: Marian C. Diamond

Initial support for the origination and publication of the GEMS series was provided by the A.W. Mellon Foundation and the Carnegie Corporation of New York. GEMS has also received support from the McDonnell-Douglas Foundation and the McDonnell-Douglas Employees Community Fund, the Hewlett Packard Company Foundation, and the people at Chevron USA. GEMS also gratefully acknowledges the contribution of word processing equipment from Apple Computer, Inc. This support does not imply responsibility for statements or views expressed in publications of the GEMS program.

Under a grant from the National Science Foundation, GEMS Leader's Workshops have been held across the country. For further information on GEMS leadership opportunities, or to receive a publication brochure and the *GEMS Network News*, please contact GEMS at the address and phone number below.

Development of this guide was sponsored in part by a grant from NSF.

Printed in the United States of America.
International Standard Book Number:
0-912511-86-9

## COMMENTS WELCOME

Great Explorations in Math and Science (GEMS) is an ongoing curriculum development project. GEMS guides are revised periodically, to incorporate teacher comments and new approaches. We welcome your criticisms, suggestions, helpful hints, and any anecdotes about your experience presenting GEMS activities. Your suggestions will be reviewed each time a GEMS guide is revised. Please send your comments to:

GEMS Revisions
Lawrence Hall of Science
University of California
Berkeley, CA 94720-5200

Our phone number is (510) 642-7771.

# Great Explorations in Math and Science (GEMS) Program

The Lawrence Hall of Science (LHS) is a public science center on the University of California at Berkeley campus. LHS offers a full program of activities for the public, including workshops and classes, exhibits, films, lectures, and special events. LHS is also a center for teacher education and curriculum research and development.

Over the years, LHS staff have developed a multitude of activities, assembly programs, classes, and interactive exhibits. These programs have proven to be successful at the Hall and should be useful to schools, other science centers, museums, and community groups. A number of these guided-discovery activities have been published under the Great Explorations in Math and Science (GEMS) title, after an extensive refinement process that includes classroom testing of trial versions, modifications to ensure the use of easy-to-obtain materials, and carefully written and edited step-by-step instructions and background information to allow presentation by teachers without special background in mathematics or science.

**Contributing GEMS/PEACHES Authors**

Jacqueline Barber
Katharine Barrett
Lincoln Bergman
Ellen Blinderman
Beatrice Boffen
Celia Cuomo
Linda De Lucchi
Jean Echols
John Erickson
Jaine Kopp
Jan M. Goodman
Alan Gould
Kimi Hosoume
Sue Jagoda
Linda Lipner
Laura Lowell
Larry Malone
Cary I. Sneider
Debra Sutter
Jennifer Meux White
Carolyn Willard

## ACKNOWLEDGMENTS

**Photographs: Richard Hoyt**

**Illustrations: Rose Craig**

Thanks to all the enthusiastic people on the PEACHES committee at the Lawrence Hall of Science—Katharine Barrett, Ellen Blinderman, Beatrice Boffen, Jean Echols, Tim Erickson, Kay Fairwell, Kimi Hosoume, Jaine Kopp, Bernadette Lauraya, Jennifer Meux White—for their many suggestions and other contributions during the development and writing of *Ladybugs*. A note of grateful appreciation goes to **Jaine Kopp**, who wrote the session on Symmetry.

We want to especially thank teachers **Linda Rogers** and **Kathy Hagerty** of the Brookfield Elementary School in Oakland, California for the generous gift of their time in helping us photograph the *Ladybugs* activities. And thanks go to the children in their kindergarten classes who graced the photographs in this guide.

# REVIEWERS

We would like to thank the following educators who reviewed, tested, or coordinated the reviewing of *this series* of GEMS/PEACHES materials in manuscript and draft form. Their critical comments and recommendations, based on presentation of these activities nationwide, contributed significantly to these GEMS publications. Their participation in the review process does not necessarily imply endorsement of the GEMS program or responsibility for statements or views expressed. Their role is an invaluable one, and their feedback is carefully recorded and integrated as appropriate into the publications.

**ALASKA**
Coordinator:
**Cynthia Dolmas Curran**

Iditarod Elementary School, Wasilla
**Cynthia Dolmas Curran**
**Christina M. Jencks**
**Beverly McPeek**
**Abby Kellner-Rode**

## CALIFORNIA

**GEMS Center, Huntington Beach**
Coordinator: **Susan Spoeneman**

College View School,
Huntington Beach
**Susan Gonzales**
**Anita Mueller**
**Elaine Ohgi**
**Sandra Silverman**
**Sandra Williamson**

Montessori Children Center,
Huntington Beach
**Erin Karal**
**LeeAnne Clokey**
**Ellen Goodman**

Haycox Elementary, Oxnard
**Margery Ann Leffingwell**

Mickelson's Family Day Care Home,
Ramona
**Levata Mickelson**

### San Francisco Bay Area
Coordinators: **Cynthia Ashley**
**Cynthia Eaton**

4C's Children's Center, Oakland
**Yolanda Coleman-Wilson**

24 Hour Children Center, Oakland
**Sheryl Lambert**
**Ella Tassin**
**Inez Watson**

Afterschool Program, Piedmont
**Willy Chen**

Alameda Head Start, Alameda
**Debbie Garcia**
**Stephanie Josey**
**Michelle Garabedian**

Albany Children's Center, Albany
**Celestine Whittaker**

Bancroft School, Berkeley
**Cecilia Saffarian**

Bartell Childcare and Learning
Center, Oakland
**Beverly Barrow**
**Barbara Terrell**

Beach Elementary School, Piedmont
**Ann Blasius**
**Juanita Forester**
**Jean Martin**
**Elodee Lessley**

Belle Vista Child Development
Center, Oakland
**Satinder Jit K. Rana**

Berkeley Head Start, Berkeley
**Marian Simmons**
**Alma Johnson**
**Xotchilt Del Carmen**
**Robinson**
**Rose Mary Wagner**

Berkeley Hills Nursery School,
Berkeley
**Elizabeth Fulton**

Berkeley-Albany YMCA, Berkeley
**Trinidad Caselis**

Berkeley/Richmond Jewish
Community, Berkeley
**Terry Amgott-Kwan**

Bernice & Joe Play School, Oakland
**Bernice Huisman-Humbert**

Bing School, Stanford
**Kate Ashbey**

Butte Kiddie Corral, Shingletown
**Cindy Stinar Black**

Brookfield Elementary School,
Oakland
**Linda Rogers,**
**Kathy Hagerty**
**Twila Richardson**

Brookfield Head Start, Oakland
**Suzie Ashley**
**Lola Hill**
**Leagun James**
**Betty Gibson**

Cedar Creek Montessori, Berkeley
**Idalina Cruz**
**Jeanne Devin**
**Len Paterson**

Centro VIda, Berkeley
**Rosalia Wilkins**

Chinese Community United
Methodist Church, Oakland
**Stella Ko Kwok**

Clayton Valley Parent Preschool,
Concord
**Lee Ann Sanders**
**Patsy Sherman**

Compañeros del Barrio State
Preschool, San Francisco
**Anastasia Decaristos**
**Laura Todd**

Contra Costa College, San Pablo
**Sylvia Alvarez-Mazzi**

Creative Learning Center, Danville
**Brooke H. B. D'Arezzo**

Creative Play Center, Pleasant Hill
**Sharon Keane**
**Debbie Coyle**

Dena's Day Care, Oakland
**Kawsar Elshinawy**

Dover Preschool, Richmond
**Alice J. Romero**

Duck's Nest Preschool, Berkeley
**Pierrette Allison**
**Patricia Foster**
**Mara Ellen Guckian**
**Ruth Major**

East Bay Community Children's Center, Oakland
**Charlotte Johnson**
**Oletha R. Wade**

Ecole Bilingue, Berkeley
**Nichelle R. Kitt**
**Martha Ann Reed**
**Richard Mermis**

Emeryville Child Development Center, Emeryville
**Ortencia A. Hoopii**
**Ellastine Blalock**
**Jonetta Bradford**
**William L. Greene**

Enrichment Plus Albert Chabot School, Oakland
**Lisa Dobbs**

Family Day Care, Oakland
**Cheryl Birden**
**Penelope Brody**
**Eufemia Buena Byrd**

Family Day Care, Orinda
**Lucy Inouye**

Gan Hillel Nursery School, Richmond
**Denise Moyes-Schnur**

Gan Shalom Preschool, Berkeley
**Iris Greenbaum**

Garner Toddler Center, Alameda
**Uma Srinath**

Gay Austin, Albany
**Sallie Hanna-Rhyne**

Giggles Family Day Care, Oakland
**Doris Wührmann**

Greater Richmond Social Services Corp., Richmond
**Lucy Coleman**

Happy Lion School, Pinole
**Sharon Espinoza**
**Marilyn Klemm**

Hawthorne Year-Round School, Oakland
**Terry Meyers**

Jack-in-the-Box Junction Preschool, Richmond
**Virginia Guadarrama**

Jewish Community Center Preschool, Walnut Creek
**Helen Hammond**

Kinder–Care, Oakland
**Terry Saugstad**

King Child Deveelopment Center, Berkeley
**Margie M. Kirk**

King Preschool, Richmond
**Charlie M. Allums**

Laney Childcare, Oakland
**Patricia Hunter**

Learning Adventures Child Development, Redding
**Dena Keown**

Longfellow Child Development Center, Oakland
**Katryna Ray**

Los Medanos Community College, Pittsburg
**Judy Henry**
**Filomena Macedo**

Maraya's Developmental Center, Oakland
**Maria A. Johnson-Price**
**Gayla Lucero**

Mark Twain School Migrant Education, Modesto
**Grace Avila**

Mary Jane's Preschool, Pleasant Hill
**Theresa Borges**

Merritt College Children's Center, Oakland
**Deborah Green**
**Virginia Shelton**

Mission Head Start, San Francisco
**Pilar Marroquin**
**Mirna Torres**

Montclair Community Play Center, Oakland
**Elaine Guttmann**
**Nancy Kliszewski**
**Mary Loeser**

Next Best Thing, Oakland
**Denise Hingle**
**Franny Minervini-Zick**

Oak Center Christian Academy, Oakland
**Debra Booze**

Oakland Parent Child Center, Oakland
**Barbara Jean Jackson**

Orinda Preschool, Orinda
**Tracy Johansing-Spittler**

Oxford St. Learning Road, Berkeley
**Vanna Maria Kalofonos**

Palma Ceia School, Hayward
**Cheryl Brush**

Peixoto Children's Center, Hayward
**Alma Arias**
**Irma Guzman**
**Paula Lawrence**
**Tyra Toney**

Piedmont Cooperative Playschool, Peidmont
**Marcia Nybakken**

Playmates Daycare, Berkeley
**Mary T. McCormick**

Rainbow School, Oakland
**Mary McCon**
**Rita Neely**

San Antonio Head Start, Oakland
**Cynthia Hammock**
**Ilda Terrazas**

San Jose City College, San Jose
**Mary Conroy**

Sequoia Nursery School, Oakland
**Karen Fong**

Sequoyah Community Preschool, Oakland
**Erin Smith**
**Kim Wilcox**

Shakelford Headstart, Modesto
**Teresa Avila**

St. Vincent's Day Home, Oakland
**Pamela Meredith**

Sunshine Preschool, Berkeley
**Poppy Richie**

The Lake School, Oakland
**Patricia House**
**Margaret Engel**
**Vickie Stoller**

The Model School Comprehensive, Berkeley
**Jenny Schwartz-Groody**

U. C. Berkeley Child Care Services Smyth Fernwald II, Berkeley
**Diane Wallace**
**Caroline W. Yee**

# REVIEWERS

Walnut Ave. Community Preschool, Walnut Creek
**Evelyn DeLanis**

Washington Child Development Center, Berkeley
**Reather Jones**

Washington Kids Club, Berkeley
**Adwoa A. Mante**

Westview Children's Center, Pacifica
**Adrienne J. Schneider**

Woodroe Woods, Hayward
**Wendy Justice**

Woodstock Child Development Center, Alameda
**Mary Raabe**

Woodstock Child Development Center, Alameda
**Denise M. Ratto**

Woodstock School, Alameda
**Amber D. Cupples**

Yuk Yan Annex, Oakland
**Eileen Lok**

YWCA Oakland, Oakland
**Iris Ezeb**
**Grace Perry**

ILLINOIS
Coordinator: **Fran Donovan**

Chicago Commons-New City Child Care Center, Chicago
**Karen Haigh**
**Andrew Clark, Jr.**
**Aurora Rodriguez**

Lake Shore School, Chicago
**Elaine Dotson**
**Louisa Economou**
**Brenda Kay Ratts**
**Karen Walsh**
**Jean Yoshimura**

MASSACHUSETTS
Coordinator: **Jeri Robinson**

Joseph P. Manning Elementary School, Jamaica Plain
**Estelle Koutoulas**
**Elynor Harrington**
**Dale Hurd**

Paige Academy, Roxbury
**Marjorie A. Jones**
**Norma Yolanda Medina**
**Florence Agatha Moving**
**Chantal Latortue Pierre**

MISSISSIPPI
Coordinator: **Johnnie Mills-Jones**

Edwards Elementary School, Edwards
**Linda Laws**
**Kimberly R. Hill**
**Sandra Pritchard**
**Margaret A. Rogers**
**Roberta Taylor**

NEW MEXICO
Coordinator: **Phyllis Etsate**

Zuni Head Start Program, Zuni
**Phyllis Etsate**
**Bernelia Boone**
**Sadie Eustace**
**Sue Tucson**

NEW YORK
Coordinator: **Marge Korzelius**

Center for the Young Child #36, Buffalo
**Sandra Jean Campbell**
**Karen Maier**
**Niris L. Campbell**
**Jeanne B. Cooley**

School 43 Annex, Buffalo
**Kathleen A. Podraza**
**Sharon R. Chapman**
**Susan L. Hoyler**
**Jessica P. Manns**

Preschool Science Collaborative, New York
**Gwendolyn Rippey**

UTAH
Coordinator: **Rose Turpin**

Mountainland Head Start, Provo
**Donna L. Rogers**
**Sheryl Schaefer**
**Glenna R. Schartmann**
**Alice Sia**

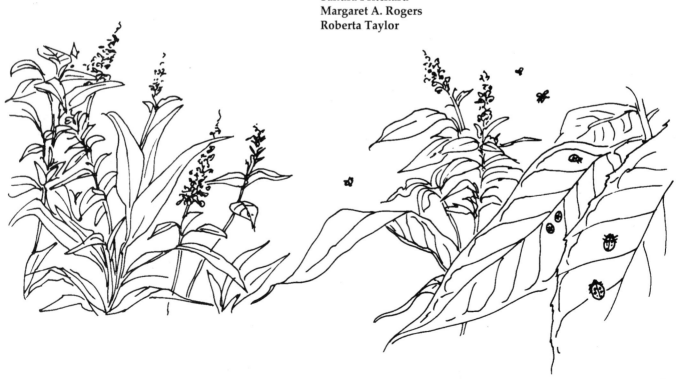

# CONTENTS

## GEMS and PEACHES

GEMS is publishing a number of early childhood activity guides developed by the PEACHES project of the Lawrence Hall of Science. PEACHES is a curriculum development and training program for teachers and parents of children in preschool through first grade.

Like the GEMS guides already available for preschool and the early grades—such as *Hide A Butterfly*, *Animal Defenses*, and *Buzzing A Hive*—the new PEACHES guides combine free exploration, drama, art, and literature with science and mathematics to give young children positive and effective learning experiences.

# INTRODUCTION

**M**any children love ladybugs and delight in finding them on leaves and flowers during the spring and summer months. They are fascinated by a ladybug's small size, round spots, and bright, shiny colors. In this series of activities, children learn about the ladybug's body structure, life cycle, defensive behavior, and favorite foods. While watching live ladybugs eat, the girls and boys discover that ladybugs help plants by devouring the tiny insects that damage plants.

*Ladybugs* teaches science concepts through observation, comparison, discussion, short drama, and role playing. Play is an important part of this unit. The children recall some of the ideas presented as they play with the paper insects they make and role-play the defensive behavior and the life cycle of the ladybug. Their play extends the learning process in an uninhibited and fun way. After completing the unit, the children take their projects home and share their dramas and role playing with their families and friends.

Math is woven into the biology of this unit. As the children learn about the anatomy of ladybugs and aphids, they count the body parts of those insects. In addition, the children are introduced to the concepts of symmetry (they look at themselves as well as other objects for symmetry, and then create symmetrical spots on paper ladybugs) and pattern (they investigate the repeating life cycle of ladybugs as they change from an egg to an adult).

Posters of ladybugs, aphids, and scale (small sucking insects that damage plants) are included so the children can see what these insects look like and learn about their body structures. However, posters can never adequately replace live insects. Letting a ladybug walk along a finger and fly away is a delightful experience. Live ladybugs, aphids, and scale to observe and enjoy add immensely to children's appreciation and understanding of insect behavior. Spring and summer are the best times of the year to present the activities in this guide since ladybugs and other insects are abundant during these seasons.

## Activities for a Wide Range of Abilities

The activities in *Ladybugs* are for children in preschool through first grade. They also can be adapted upward for second and

Ladybug, Ladybug
Don't fly away
Your home is my garden
I want you to stay
With your eggs
And your babies
This bright sunny day
Stay in my garden
Where we can play.

third graders. Because of a wide range of abilities, some of the activities are more appropriate for younger children and others for older students. It is not necessary to do every activity with each age group.

The lesson descriptions include suggestions for modifying the activities to make them appropriate for the level of your students. For younger children, you may want to limit the activities on the ladybug life cycle to Activity 3: Eggs and Baby Ladybugs. Children in preschool and kindergarten enjoy learning that ladybugs lay eggs and seeing what baby ladybugs look like. Children in first grade can continue with Activity 4: Ladybug Pupae and Life Cycle and learn about the change that occurs in the ladybug during its pupal stage.

Activity 5: Ladybugs Rescue the Orange Trees may be more appropriate for children in kindergarten and first grade. The idea of using ladybugs instead of insecticides is highlighted in a dramatic way, which a child this age can understand and appreciate. Some of the concepts may be too abstract for many preschool children. On the other hand, introducing these ideas to preschoolers in appropriate ways can provide a basis, and challenge, for future learning. The same is true of the life cycle concepts.

For preschoolers, select activities that children can experience firsthand: tasting, seeing, touching, and role playing. Keep the activities short and introduce fewer concepts, facts, and new words in each session. Older children can handle more discussion and more detailed observations.

## Choices

Not only are there choices of activities to do with the children, but there are also choices about how to present them. Depending on your teaching approach and the skills of the children, you may choose to have the youngsters design their own ladybugs and aphids or use the paper cutouts that encourage the children to focus on the body structure of these insects.

## Notes on Use of This Book

- Often we include questions to ask the children; the answers to the questions are included after the question in brackets and italics *[brackets and italics]*. Directions, such as make your hand look like a bird are included in parentheses (make your hand look like a bird).

- The full-page illustrations in the book are reproduced at the back of the book and perforated so you can tear them out for easy duplication.

- If you are working with children too young to use scissors you can do any necessary cutouts beforehand and have the materials ready for the children's activity.

- At the back of the book on page 77 are Summary Outlines of all the activities, which you can use as a quick reminder when you present the activities.

- As you present the activities you may wish to refer to the Literature Connections on page 76, which give suggestions of children's literature that contains themes and situations relevant to a particular activity. These books could be read aloud during that activity.

— *ACTIVITY 1* —

# GETTING TO KNOW LADYBUGS

## Overview

Learning about ladybugs generates enthusiasm for these color-ful insects. The children observe live ladybugs and posters of ladybugs to learn about their behavior and body structure. As the children look at the posters and make paper ladybugs, they find out that ladybugs have six legs, two antennae, two flying wings, and two cover wings. They take part in dramatic and role-playing activities to show some of the fascinating ways ladybugs protect themselves from birds.

The children learn about symmetry as they discover the symmetry in their bodies and a ladybug's body. They continue their exploration of symmetry through a variety of art projects. The boys and girls also create symmetrical spots on ladybug draw-ings, which provide an opportunity to practice counting skills as well as to make guesses about numbers.

## *Session 1*

# INTRODUCING LADYBUGS

## WHAT YOU NEED

### For the whole group

➤ 1 Ladybug poster
➤ 1 Flying Ladybug poster
➤ 1 red marker, or red watercolor paint and a brush
➤ Pictures of ladybugs (See Resource Books on page 75 for books with color illustrations and photographs of lady-bugs.)

### For each child and yourself

➤ 1 clear plastic container, such as a plastic cup, with a lid or a bug box
➤ 1 live ladybug (The value of having live ladybugs for the children to observe and enjoy is well worth the time and

the small amount of money you spend. You can buy ladybugs from a biological supply company or from most garden supply stores during the spring and summer months, if you cannot collect them in your area. See Resource Materials on page 75.)

### For caring for the ladybugs

➤ 1 clear plastic or glass container, such as a fish bowl
➤ 1 piece of nylon stocking
➤ 1 rubber band
➤ 1 small bunch of plant leaves and stems that are covered with aphids (Look on rose bushes, dandelions, nasturtiums, strawberry, bean, pea, and tomato plants.)
➤ 1 spray bottle

#### Optional
➤ 1 small yogurt container with a lid
➤ 1 sharp knife or pair of scissors

## GETTING READY

### Anytime Before the Activity

1. It is useful to learn more about ladybugs before you begin these activities in case the children ask you any unanticipated questions. Background Information on page 72 tells you about ladybug body structure, life cycle, defenses, and the insects ladybugs eat. Many excellent books with information about ladybugs are available. Some are referenced on page 75.

2. Color the Ladybug and Flying Ladybug posters to make them more attractive and realistic.

3. If aphids or a commercial ladybug food are unavailable, keep the ladybugs in the warmest part of the refrigerator until you are ready to use them. Refrigeration slows down their movements and metabolism so much that they do not eat. If aphids are available, follow these steps:

   a. Place several plant leaves and stems that are covered with aphids in the container.

   b. Lightly mist the leaves and stems. Be careful not to let much water collect on the bottom of the container because ladybugs can drown in very little water.

   c. Put the ladybugs into the container.

➤ *If you decide to place the plants in water to keep them fresh longer, you need to cover the water so the ladybugs won't fall in and drown. An easy way to do this is to fill a yogurt cup with water, put the lid on the cup, poke a few holes in the lid, and push the stems through the holes. Place the cup with the plants in the container.*

d. Cover the mouth of the container with a piece of nylon stocking.

e. Use a rubber band to hold the stocking in place.

f. Remove the wilted plants daily, put freshly cut plants in the container, and mist the leaves and stems. You can mist the plants through the nylon stocking.

g. If you have a large supply of aphids, you can keep the ladybugs in the container for a week or more.

4. Keep the container of ladybugs in the room for the children to observe.

5. Look outside for a safe place for the girls and boys to release some of the ladybugs, preferably an area with plants and bushes that are covered with aphids. After releasing the ladybugs, the children may find them in the area for weeks. Also, they may find ladybug eggs, larvae, and pupae after two or three weeks.

➤ *Ladybugs become very active when they are warm. If you need to open the container to feed or move the ladybugs, put the container in the warmest part of the refrigerator for a few hours to slow down the ladybugs.*

## Immediately Before the Activity

1. Place the live ladybugs in containers with lids, one ladybug to a container for each child to observe. The children will release some of the ladybugs at the end of this activity.

2. Place the ladybugs and both posters in the section of the room where you present the activity.

## Observing Live Ladybugs

1. Gather the children in a circle on the floor and say, "I'm thinking of a very tiny animal that's red with black spots. Guess what it is." *[A ladybug]*

2. Give each child a ladybug in a container with a lid. Caution the children to hold the containers gently so they won't hurt the ladybugs. Ask questions that encourage careful observations, such as:

   • "What is your ladybug doing?"

   • "What colors do you see on your ladybug?"

   • "Does your ladybug have any spots?"

3. Tell the boys and girls to look under the containers to see what the ladybugs look like from underneath.

4. Collect the containers and put them aside so that the children can observe and release the ladybugs later.

## Observing the Ladybug Poster

1. Show the Ladybug poster, and encourage the children to talk about their experiences with ladybugs.

2. Ask the group to count with you as you point to the six legs, two eyes, and two feelers on the ladybug poster. (Use the word *antennae* if you think it is appropriate for your group.)

3. Ask the youngsters:

   - "What do you use when you touch things?" *[Fingers]*
   - "What do you use to smell things?" *[Nose]*

4. Ask the children if they know how ladybugs touch and smell. Tell them ladybugs use their feelers for touching and smelling things.

## Observing the Flying Ladybug Poster

1. Show the Flying Ladybug poster. Let the children guess what the ladybug is doing. Tell them that the ladybug has two kinds of wings.

   - The wings with spots are hard. They are called *cover wings* because they cover the back of the ladybug and protect it. Ask a child to point to a cover wing.
   - The other wings are called *flying wings.* Ladybugs move them when they fly. Have a child point to a flying wing. Ask if anyone saw the flying wings on the live ladybug.

2. Ask the children to count with you as you point to the two flying wings and the two cover wings. Tell the group that the ladybug lifts its cover wings up out of the way when it flies, and keeps them very still.

## Ladybug Pictures

1. Have ladybug books in the room so the children can look at the color photographs and illustrations of ladybugs.

## Ladybug Hunt

1. Take the children outside to look for ladybugs.

2. Encourage them to look on flowers, leaves, grass, and in the air.

## Ladybug Role Play

1. While outside, let the boys and girls pretend they are ladybugs flying.

2. The children can crawl on the ground and pretend they have six legs.

## Letting Live Ladybugs Fly Away

1. While outside, give each child one live ladybug in a container with a lid. Tell the children to look again at the ladybugs and find the ladybug legs and feelers.

2. Encourage the children to lift the lids off the containers and to let the ladybugs crawl on their hands. Remind the youngsters to be very gentle with the ladybugs.

3. If a ladybug leaves a bad smell on a child's hand, tell the group that ladybugs sometimes make bad smells to protect them-selves so that they will be left alone. Ladybugs also taste bad, and sometimes birds won't eat them because of the bad taste.

4. Tell the group to look for the flying wings and the cover wings as the ladybugs fly away.

**Note:** Keep or recapture several ladybugs for later activities. Try to keep at least three ladybugs with six or fewer spots for the activity Symmetry on page 19.

➤ *If squeezed, ladybugs can bite, but their bites are not dangerous.*

# GOING FURTHER

1. Show pictures of other types of ladybugs, such as brown ladybugs with white spots or ladybugs with no spots.

2. Put out paper, paint, and paint brushes to give the children an opportunity to paint imaginative ladybugs.

3. Encourage each child to make several paintings. To assess how much the children learned about ladybugs, keep one painting from each child. At the end of this unit, have the children paint ladybugs again and ask them to describe what they have painted. Compare the first paintings with the recent ones.

*Session 2*

# SYMMETRY

## A Preliminary Note About Symmetry

The activities in this session are meant as an intuitive level introduction to symmetry for young children. The children explore bilateral symmetry in the following symmetry activities. Bilateral symmetry can be illustrated by folding a sheet of paper in half—the fold line that divides the paper into two equal halves is the line of symmetry. The section on either side of the line matches its opposite exactly. Not all objects have a line of symmetry—not all can be divided into equal matching halves. The spots on a ladybug and many external features of the human body are examples of symmetry.

## WHAT YOU NEED

### For the group

➤ 1 piece of yarn 4' long
➤ 1 ladybug poster

#### Optional
➤ Several plastic containers with one ladybug in each

### For each child and yourself

➤ 1 Ladybug Spots sheet on page 28
➤ 1 small paintbrush or a cotton swab

### For each pair of children and yourself

➤ 1 small container of black paint
➤ Art supplies: paper, scissors, crayons, felt pens, hole punch

## GETTING READY

1. Set out paint at each table along with either a cotton swab or a paintbrush for each child.

2. Select an art activity to do with your children and set out the appropriate materials.

3. You may want to pre-fold the Ladybug Spots sheet along the center line.

## Symmetry and Me

1. Ask one child to volunteer to stand up in front of the group. Tell the children to imagine a line drawn down the middle of the child from head to toe. Hold a piece of yarn in front of the child as shown in the illustration on the next page.

2. Point out the eye on each side of the yarn. Ask the children what other things are the *same on each side* of the yarn. (Ears, nostrils, eyebrows, hands, arms, toes, legs, knees, feet, etc.— this is a good time to identify and label body parts.)

3. Depending upon your children's level of development, you may want to introduce the word ***symmetry***. If you do, explain that some parts of their body have symmetry — they look basically the same on each side of the yarn.

4. Now put the yarn across the volunteer's waist. Look at both sides of the yarn. Ask if the child is the same on both sides of the yarn. *[No]* Ask, "If we fold you at your waist, what will your head touch?" Although a line across the waist is not a line of symmetry, it is helpful to explore the possibility so that children see that only one line divides the body symmetrically.

5. Pair the children and encourage them to make observations about their bodies. Ask questions such as

   • "What is the same on both sides of your partner's face?" *[Eyes, Ears]*

   • "What is the same on both of your partner's legs?" *[Knees, Feet]*

6. If appropriate for your children, look at various objects in the classroom and check for symmetry. For example, choose a symmetrical toy animal. Place the yarn down the line of symmetry on the animal. Have the children identify the parts that are the same on both sides of the yarn. Look at other classroom materials such as dolls, model vehicles, clothing in the dress-up corner, or the children's clothing.

➤ *Children may notice things that are not parts of the body that are not the same, such as a bracelet on only one hand or a hole in one pant knee. Some children may note more subtle differences in size or appearance between, for example, two ears or eyebrows. Acknowledge these accurate observations. (While many, but not all, of the main external physical features of humans do have a basic symmetry, it is certainly not exact, and the internal structures of the human body are often not symmetrical. The object of this part of the activity is to provide young children with a basic sense of what symmetry means and some ways in which their own bodies may reflect this concept.)*

➤ *When looking at clothing, the article itself may be symmetrical though the way it is decorated may not be. For example, a pullover sweater with a pocket only on one side may give rise to a discussion on symmetry. Some children may see the sweater as symmetrical, while others will argue that it is not. It is not as important to classify the sweater as symmetrical or not symmetrical as it is to listen to your children's thinking and observations, and to validate all their classification efforts.*

## Symmetry Art Activities

Three different art activities that will help the children understand the concept of symmetry are below. You may want to do only one or perhaps all the activities depending on your children's skills and abilities. You may decide to have the children do the activities in small groups over several days and again as free choice activities following Ladybug Symmetry. Remember, it is the process that is important. It is fine if the artwork is not completely symmetrical. These activities will give the children an intuitive understanding of symmetry that they will explore in greater depth in later years.

### • Squish Paintings

Paint a picture. Fold the paper in half and press down. Open it and look at the two symmetrical sides. For a more dramatic effect, children may want to cut out their favorite design and paste it on a colored sheet of paper.

### • Cutouts

Fold a sheet of paper in half. Cut out a free-form shape from the edge of the folded side of the paper. Open up the paper and observe that the shapes on both sides are the same! Suggest to the children that they decorate the sides symmetrically with crayons, felt pens, or pencils. Older children may cut simple shapes including butterflies, hearts, and ovals, as well as making additional cuts in each of the sides of their shapes.

### • Hole Punches

Fold a sheet of paper in half. Punch several holes in the folded sheet. Open it up and observe where the holes are. Suggest to the children that they decorate around the holes symmetrically.

## Ladybug Symmetry

1. Ask the children if they think a ladybug's body is the same on both sides (symmetrical).

2. Give a copy of the Ladybugs Spots sheet to each child. Have the children fold the sheet on the line to create a clear line of symmetry. Keep in mind that the fold does not need to be done exactly! Help those children who need assistance folding.

➤ *Some children may not make exactly round spots on the ladybug. That is fine! The shapes will be duplicated symmetrically when folded. Some children may paint spots on both ladybug wings. Again, when they fold the Ladybug sheet, the resulting spots will be symmetrical.*

3. Ask the children to look at each side of the ladybug. What things are the same on both sides? *[Antennae, eyes, legs, wings, wing covers]*

4. What is the ladybug missing? *[Spots]* Tell the children that they are going to put spots on their ladybugs.

5. Show the children how to paint dots on one wing on one side of the ladybug using a cotton swab or small paintbrush. Count the dots. Then fold the paper on the line of symmetry. Before you open the paper ask the children to guess how many dots will be on the other wing. Accept all guesses. Ask, "How many dots will there be on the ladybug altogether?" Open the sheet and count!

6. Have the children go to tables to make their ladybug spots.

7. Have the children count the spots they paint on one of the ladybug's wings. Fold the sheet on the line and then open it. How many spots are there now on both wings?

8. If available, have the children look at live ladybugs, or the large poster, to see if the number of spots are the same on both wings.

## Going Further

1. Let the children repeat the symmetry art activities.

2. Have the children use their Ladybug Spots sheets and their symmetry art work to create Symmetry Books.

*Session 3*

# MAKING PAPER LADYBUGS

## Choices For Making Ladybugs

The children make paper ladybugs and use them in a series of creative-play activities. Depending on your teaching approach and the skills of the children, you may choose to have the children make very simple ladybugs, design their own ladybugs, or follow the directions for making ladybugs that focus on ladybug body structure.

## The Simple Ladybug

Three-year-old children can make very simple paper ladybugs by gluing on legs, sticking on dots, and drawing features. (See the drawing on this page.)

It is not important that these creations look like ladybugs. The placement of the legs, dots, and features reflect a young child's vision. The child is just beginning to observe nature and express what she sees, understands, and imagines.

The children need large oval shapes cut from red construction paper, strips of black construction paper, black markers, and black stick-and-peel dots.

## The Child-Designed Ladybug

If the children have the skills, let them design, cut out, and assemble their own ladybugs. These ladybugs may be somewhat realistic or very imaginative. The purpose of this approach is to encourage the children's creativity and promote their independence.

The girls and boys need sheets of red, black, and white construction paper, scissors, paste, and black crayons or markers.

## The Ladybug Model

Making ladybug models encourages the children to make ladybugs that have six legs, two antennae, two cover wings, and two flying wings. In the process of assembling the parts, the children learn about the body structure of the ladybug. Although this approach is structured, it allows for individual expression in the placement of the body parts. No two ladybugs ever look alike.

If you select this approach, you need to prepare the materials in advance. See the What You Need, Getting Ready, and Making Ladybug Models sections that follow.

## WHAT YOU NEED

### For the whole group

➤ 1 tray
➤ Newspaper, enough to cover the tray and work tables

### For each child and yourself

➤ 1 sheet of 6" x 6" black construction paper
➤ 1 sheet of 4" x 4" white paper
➤ 1 sheet of 5" x 5" red construction paper
➤ 1 black crayon or marker
➤ 1 white crayon or chalk
➤ 1 container of white paste or glue

## GETTING READY

### Anytime Before the Activity

1. Using the patterns on page 31, cut out one ladybug for each child and one for yourself. For each ladybug cut out:
   ➤ One ladybug body (pattern A) out of black paper
   ➤ Six legs (pattern D) out of black paper
   ➤ Two antennae (pattern E) out of black paper
   ➤ Two cover wings (pattern B) out of red paper
   ➤ Two flying wings (pattern C) out of white paper

### Immediately Before the Activity

1. Place one paper ladybug body, six legs, one pair of flying wings, one pair of cover wings, two antennae, one black crayon, one white crayon, paste, and newspaper on a tray.

2. Put the tray in the section of the room where you present the activities.

3. Spread newspaper on the tables and place one ladybug body, six legs, the crayons, and paste at each child's work place.

4. Place the antennae and wings nearby to distribute when the children are ready for them.

## Making Ladybug Models

1. Gather the children in a circle on the floor, and have them help you make a paper ladybug.

    • Write your name on the underside of the ladybug's body using a white crayon.

    • Ask the children to count the body parts with you as you glue on the legs, flying wings, cover wings, and antennae.

    • Ask, "What else does this ladybug need?" *[Eyes, Mouth, Spots]* Use a black crayon to draw the eyes, mouth, and spots.

2. Have the children make their own ladybugs.

3. After the children have glued on the legs, distribute the flying wings and then the cover wings.

4. Encourage the children to use the word feelers (or *antennae*) when they ask for the feelers as you distribute them.

➢ *Having the children assist you in making the ladybug provides important review for the children and feedback for you.*

*Session 4*

# LADYBUG DEFENSES

## WHAT YOU NEED

### For the whole group

➤ 1 brown, tan, green, or grey blanket, sheet, or bedspread

### For each child and yourself

➤ 1 black peel-and-stick dot

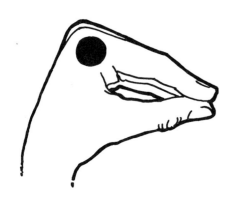

### A Ladybug Enemy

1. In a circle, tell the children that some birds eat ladybugs. Pretend that one of your hands is a hungry bird looking for something to eat. (Hold your four fingers together and your thumb under the fingers to make your hand look like a bird's head. Place a black sticker on your hand for an eye.)

2. Ask the children, "What do you think a ladybug would do if a bird came too close to it?" [*Fly away*]

   • Place a paper ladybug on the floor in front of you.

   • Move your hand "bird" over to the ladybug.

   • Have the ladybug fly away.

3. Tell the group that sometimes a ladybug gets away from a bird by dropping out of a tree and lying on its back. Then the ladybug stays very still, and the bird doesn't see it.

4. Hold one of your arms out in a horizontal position and pretend it is a tree branch. Use the "branch" (your arm), the "bird" (your hand), and a paper ladybug to present a short drama about ladybug defenses. Tell the story as you move the ladybug and then the bird on and off the branch.

   • A ladybug crawls onto a branch. What do you think eats ladybugs?

   • A bird flies toward the ladybug. The hungry bird is looking for something to eat. It sees the ladybug.

   • The bird opens its beak to eat the ladybug.

   • Just then the ladybug drops off the branch (move your arm to make the ladybug fall off your arm), falls to the ground, and lies on its back.

- The surprised bird looks on the branch and under the branch but it can't find the ladybug.

- The bird flies away to look for something else to eat.

5. Ask, "Why didn't the bird eat the ladybug?" *[Because the bird couldn't find the ladybird. The bird was looking on the branch and the ladybug was lying very still on the ground]*

## Role-Playing the Defenses of a Ladybug

1. Take the children outside and spread a blanket on the ground. Gather your group on the blanket and tell the children to pretend that they are ladybugs on a "branch" (blanket).

2. Pretend to be a hungry bird flying toward the branch.

3. Ask, "What do the ladybugs do when the bird comes close to the branch?" Encourage the children to "fly" away or roll off the blanket and onto the ground.

4. Tell them to lie on the ground like a ladybug. (On their backs and very still.)

5. If a child lies quietly on the ground near the blanket say, "The bird doesn't see that ladybug because it is staying very still." If a child keeps moving say, "The bird would find this ladybug because it keeps moving."

6. When all of the children move off the blanket say, "The hungry bird doesn't see any ladybugs on the branch. It flies away to find something else to eat."

7. "Fly" away from the branch and the ladybugs.

## More Drama

1. Back inside, distribute the children's paper ladybugs and a black sticker to each child to use as a bird's eye. Encourage the children to use their ladybugs and their "birds" to reenact the drama of ladybugs dropping off branches and laying on their backs, or flying away when a hungry bird approaches.

2. Tell the children that they will leave their paper ladybugs in the room for a few days because they will make leaf homes for their ladybugs.

➤ *One teacher collected smooth, oval-shaped rocks and let the children paint them to look like ladybugs. The results were delightful.*

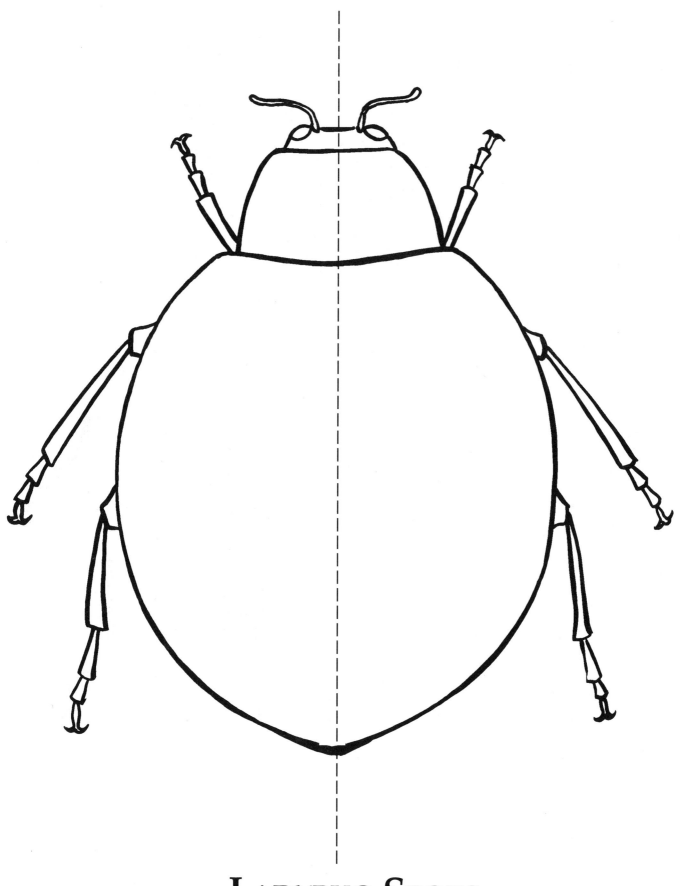

# Ladybug Spots

# LADYBUG

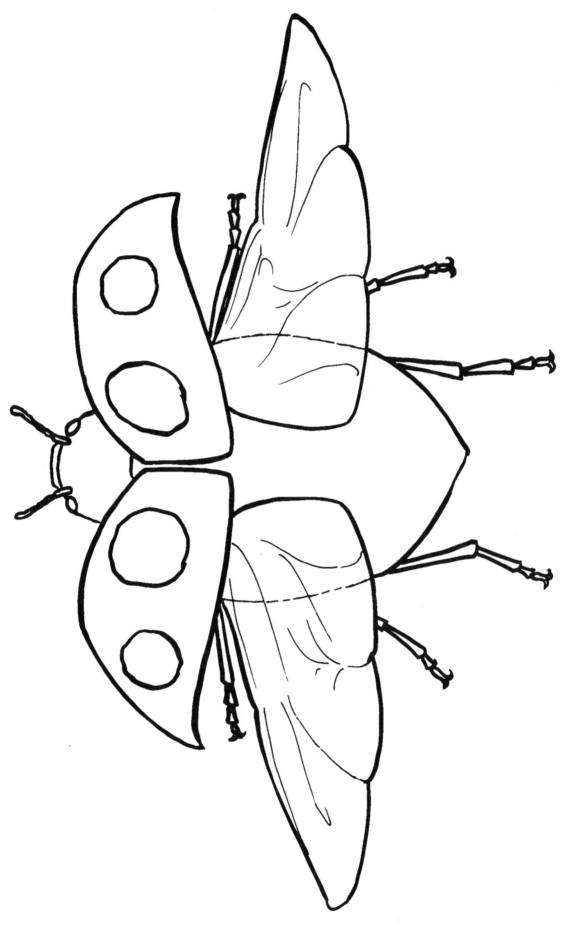

# FLYING LADYBUG

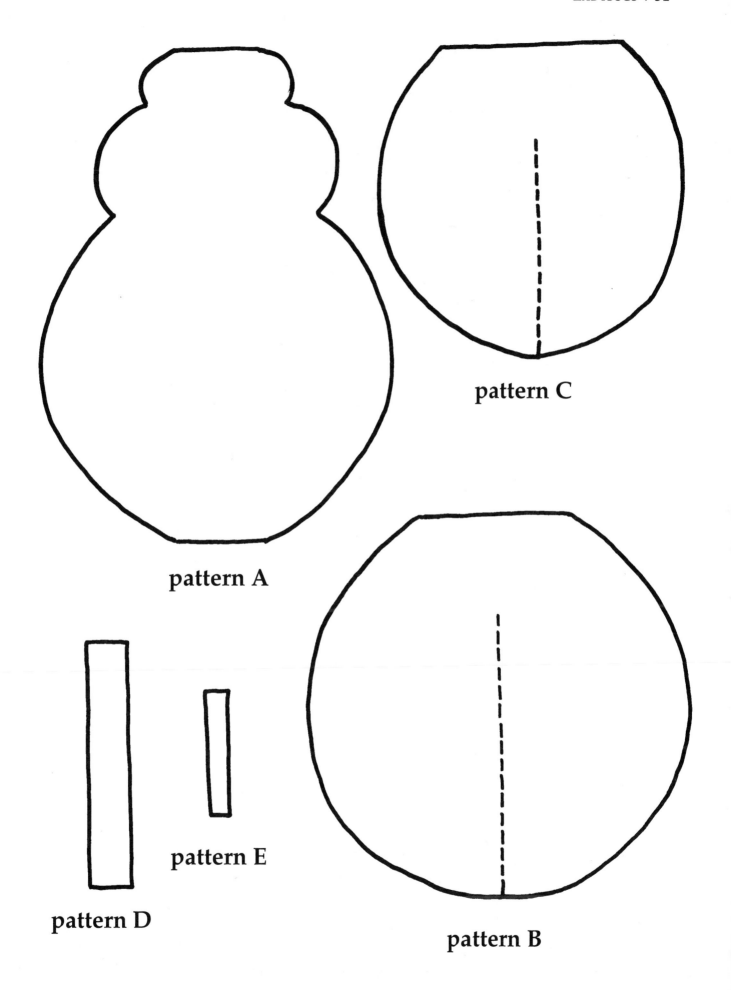

pattern C

pattern A

pattern E

pattern D

pattern B

## — *Activity 2* —

# LADYBUGS EATING APHIDS

## Overview

The children learn that ladybugs eat aphids—tiny animals that feed on plants. Wearing white ladybug flying wings and spotted cover wings, the boys and girls pretend they are ladybugs and eat "aphid" popsicles. They make paper leaves and aphids, and place the aphids on the leaves for their ladybugs to eat.

> ➤ *One teacher thought her first graders would find wearing ladybug wings babyish, but the children loved it.*

## *Session 1*

# LADYBUGS, PLANTS, AND APHIDS

## WHAT YOU NEED

### For the whole group

- ➤ 1 Ladybug Eating Aphids poster
- ➤ 1 stapler
- ➤ 1 pair of scissors
- ➤ 1 store-bought or homemade orange popsicle (To make popsicles, see Homemade Popsicles on page 34.)
- ➤ 1 tray
- ➤ 1 12" x 18" sheet of green paper
- ➤ 1 12" x 18" sheet of waxed paper
- ➤ 1 role of double-stick tape
- ➤ 3 clear plastic containers with lids
- ➤ Live aphids on leaves (See page 73 for information on finding aphids.)
- ➤ Pictures of aphids (See Resource Books on page 75 for books with color photographs and drawings of aphids.)
- ➤ Live ladybugs

### For each child and yourself

- ➤ 2 sheets of 9" x 12" red construction paper
- ➤ 2 sheets of 9" x 12" white tissue, waxed, or construction paper
- ➤ 1 sheet of 4" x 4" orange construction paper (cut a few extra sheets)
- ➤ 1 piece of black or red yarn , approximately 2½ feet long

#### Optional
- ➤ 1 hand lens

> *Instead of an aphid popsicle, one teacher suggested using raisins or dabs of peanut butter on a celery stick to represent aphids on a branch.*

# HOMEMADE POPSICLES

## WHAT YOU NEED

### For the whole group

> 1 container of orange juice, enough for each child to have one 3-ounce cup

### For each child and yourself

> 1 paper cup, 3-ounce size

> 1 popsicle stick (or craft stick found in craft stores and some drug stores)

### Getting Ready

Prepare one orange juice popsicle for each child and yourself.

1. Pour orange juice into the paper cups until the cups are three-quarters full.

2. Place the cups in the freezer until the juice is half-frozen.

3. Put a popsicle stick into the center of each cup of half-frozen juice.

4. Place the cups back in the freezer.

5. Immediately before the activity, take the cups of frozen juice out of the freezer. Keep them at room temperature for a few minutes to make it easier to lift the popsicles out of the cups.

## GETTING READY

### Anytime Before the Activity

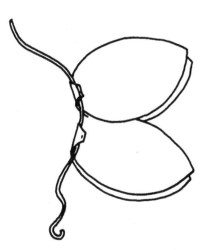

> *If the children are skilled with scissors, let them cut out their wings. You can help them assemble the wings.*

1. Make two paper ladybug cover wings with the red construction paper and two flying wings with the white paper for each child in your group. (See the drawing on this page.) For each child do the following:

   • Cut four large oval shapes—two white wings and two red cover wings. (You can stack the paper and cut four ovals at one time.)

   • Place the white wings on top of the red cover wings.

- Fold over about one-half inch of paper at the top of each set of wings.
- Place the yarn under the folds, and staple the tops down.

2. Use the patterns on page 41 to cut one aphid body (pattern K) out of orange paper for each child and yourself. Cut out a few extra aphid bodies in case some get wet and tear.

3. Bend the aphid legs down and the antennae up.

4. Write the children's names on the aphids if you plan to use them again in Making Aphids on page 38.

## Immediately Before the Activity

1. Use double-stick tape to attach one paper aphid body to each popsicle stick.

2. Place a sheet of green paper on a tray and a sheet of waxed paper over the green paper. Take the aphid popsicles out of the cups and put them on the waxed paper.

3. Put the tray back in the freezer until the children are ready to eat the popsicles.

## Observing Live Aphids and Ladybugs

**Note:** If you don't have live aphids, show drawings or photographs of aphids and of ladybugs eating aphids.

1. Show the children a live aphid, and give them plenty of time to look for these delicate little insects on the leaves you collected.

2. Tell the boys and girls that aphids suck juices from plants. When there are hundreds of aphids on the plants, the plants may turn brown and die.

3. Have the children hunt for leaves that have brown spots. Ask, "Are there any aphids on the leaves with brown spots?"

4. Say, "Pretend we have a garden and there are aphids on the plants in our garden. We don't want the plants to die. What could we do?" Encourage the children to make suggestions. If they mention spraying the plants you could suggest, "Let's find another way to get rid of the aphids."

➤ *If your group has experience with hand lenses, let the youngsters use lenses to find the aphids.*

5. Put ladybugs, aphids, and leaves in clear plastic containers with lids. Encourage the children to watch and see if the ladybugs eat the aphids.

6. As a review ask, "What do aphids eat?" *[Juices from leaves]* "What eats aphids?" *[Ladybugs]* "How do ladybugs help plants?" *[They eat the aphids that hurt the plants]*

## Observing the Poster and Nature

1. Show the Ladybug Eating Aphids poster to the children. Ask, "What do you think is happening in this picture?" Allow time for the youngsters to talk about the poster.

2. Have a child count an aphid's legs and feelers.

3. Ask, "How do you think the aphid uses its feelers?" *[To smell and touch]*

4. Take the children outside and have them hunt for aphids and ladybugs.

## "Ladybugs" Eating Aphid Popsicles

1. Back inside in the circle, tell the children they are going to pretend to be ladybugs and wear paper ladybug wings. Show them how to decorate the ladybug cover wings.

   • Write your name on one cover wing.

   • Draw large black dots on both cover wings.

2. Send the children to the tables to write their names and decorate their ladybug cover wings.

3. Tie the wings on the children.

4. Take the group outside, and encourage the "ladybugs" to "fly" around the yard and look for aphids.

5. Ask the "ladybugs" if they would like to eat aphids. Bring out the tray of "aphids" (orange juice popsicles) for the children to eat.

6. Help the children remove their wings and keep them for more role-playing activities.

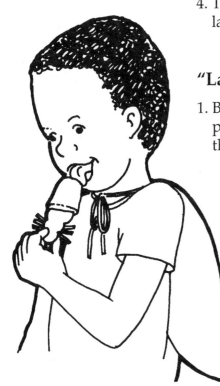

➤ *After the children finish eating their popsicles, take the aphid bodies off the popsicle sticks and keep them in the room for the activity Making Paper Aphids.*

*Session 2*

# MAKING LEAF HOMES

### Choices For Making Leaves

The children need paper leaves for later creative-play activities. You may want to pre-cut the leaves for very young preschoolers. For children who can make their own leaves, see the What You Need, Getting Ready, and Making Paper Leaves sections that follow.

## WHAT YOU NEED

### For each child and yourself

➤ 1 sheet of 9" x 12" green construction paper
➤ 1 pair of scissors
➤ 1 black crayon or marker

## GETTING READY

1. Put one green sheet of paper, scissors, and a black crayon at each child's work place.

### Making Paper Leaves

1. Have the children make paper leaves that are bigger than their ladybugs.

   • Show the children who are just learning to use scissors how to snip the corners off a green sheet of paper to make a leaf. Then have them make their own leaves.

   • Let the boys and girls, who like to draw and can cut curves, design and cut out their own leaves.

2. Be sure the children's names are on their leaves, and keep them in the room for later activities.

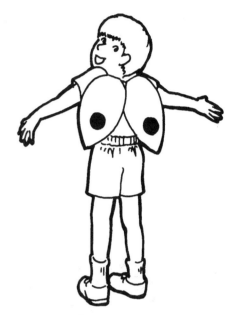

➤ *A kindergarten teacher told us two children in her class wore ladybug wings for Halloween.*

*Session 3*

# MAKING APHIDS

### Choices For Making Aphids

In this activity, the children use their paper aphids for creative-play activities. They may pretend the hungry paper ladybugs eat or fail to catch the escaping aphids.

The youngsters can draw aphids on their paper leaves or make aphids by gluing a paper aphid abdomen onto a paper aphid body. If you want the children to glue the aphid cutouts together, see the What You Need, Getting Ready, and Making Paper Aphids sections that follow.

## WHAT YOU NEED

### For the group

➤ 1 pair of scissors
➤ 1 tray
➤ Newspaper, enough to cover the tray and work tables

### For each child and yourself

➤ 1 leaf (made in Session 2: Making Leaf Homes on page 37)
➤ 1 paper ladybug (made in Activity 1: Getting to Know Ladybugs on page 13)
➤ 1 paper aphid body (made in Session 1: Ladybugs, Plants, and Aphids on page 33)
➤ 1 sheet of 2" x 2" orange construction paper
➤ 1 black crayon or marker
➤ 1 container of white paste or glue

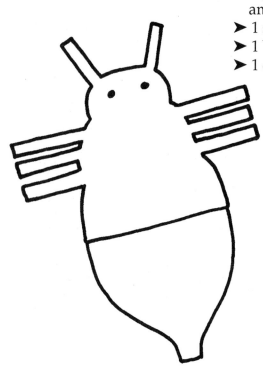

## GETTING READY

### Anytime Before the Activity

1. Use pattern L on page 41 to cut one aphid abdomen out of orange paper for each child and yourself.

## Immediately Before the Activity

1. Place one paper aphid body, one paper aphid abdomen, one black crayon, paste, and newspaper on a tray. Put the tray in the area where you present the activity.

2. Spread newspaper on the tables. Put paste, one black crayon, and one paper aphid abdomen at each child's work place.

## Making Paper Aphids

1. Show the boys and girls how to make a paper aphid by pasting the paper aphid abdomen onto the body.

2. Ask, "How many legs does the aphid have?" *[Six]* Along with the children, count the aphid's six legs.

3. Ask, "What does the aphid have on its head that it uses to touch and smell?" *[Feelers]*

4. Ask, "What does the aphid need on its face?" *[Eyes, Mouth]* Have a child draw eyes and a mouth on the aphid.

5. Distribute paper aphid bodies to the children and have them go to the tables to make their aphids.

## Creative Play

1. Give the children their leaves, aphids, and ladybugs.

2. Allow time for the children to play freely with their projects. The youngsters may pretend the ladybugs are eating the aphids or the aphids are hiding under the leaves, or running away.

3. Tell the children they will leave their ladybugs, leaves, and aphids in the room because they will make baby ladybugs to live on the leaves.

# LADYBUG EATING APHIDS

pattern K

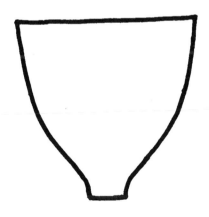

pattern L

# APHID

# — *Activity 3* —
# EGGS AND BABY LADYBUGS

## Overview

The children learn that ladybug babies hatch from eggs, eat aphids, and grow bigger. By observing live ladybug larvae or larvae pictures, the group discovers that baby ladybugs look very different from their parents. The children watch dramas, add eggs to their paper leaves, make baby ladybugs, and role-play the first two stages in a ladybug's life cycle.

For information on the specific steps in the ladybug life cycle, see Life Cycle in Background Information on page 72.

## Modifications For Very Young Children

Since ladybug larvae look so different from adult ladybugs, very young children find it hard to believe that these strange-looking creatures are ladybugs. You may choose to use the words "baby ladybug" instead of the word *larva* to reinforce the idea that these wingless creatures are ladybugs.

You may decide not to have this young age group make baby ladybugs. Instead, have the girls and boys add eggs to their leaves and guess what baby ladybugs look like. Then show them color photographs and illustrations of ladybug eggs and larvae.

*Session 1*

# LADYBUG EGGS

## Choices For Making Ladybug Eggs

In this session, the children pretend a paper ladybug lays eggs on their leaves. The boys and girls can either draw eggs or glue yellow paper eggs onto their leaves. If they use paper eggs, read the What You Need and Getting Ready sections that follow.

## WHAT YOU NEED

### For the whole group

➤ 1 paper ladybug
➤ 1 pair of scissors
➤ Newspaper, enough to cover the work tables

### For each child and yourself

➤ 1 paper leaf with an aphid
➤ 1 sheet of 1" x 1½" yellow construction paper
➤ 1 container of white paste or glue

## GETTING READY

### Anytime Before the Activity

1. Cut one or more eggs (Pattern F on page 50) out of yellow paper for each child and yourself.

### Immediately Before the Activity

1. Spread newspaper on the tables. Place one paper leaf, with the child's name showing, and some paste at each child's work place.

2. Have the ladybug eggs near the tables to distribute when the children are ready for them.

3. Have one paper ladybug, one paper leaf with an aphid, one paper ladybug egg, and paste in the area where you present the drama.

## Egg Laying Drama

1. Gather the children in a circle on the floor, and place the paper leaf with an egg and an aphid in the middle of the circle. Have the egg hidden under the leaf, the aphid on top of the leaf, and the ladybug nearby.

2. Use the leaf, aphid, egg, and paper ladybug to present a short drama.

   • A mother ladybug flies in the sky looking for an aphid on a leaf. Do you see an aphid? (Ask a child to point to the aphid.)

   • The mother is about to lay her eggs. She wants her babies to have something to eat when they crawl out of their eggs. What could a baby ladybug eat on this leaf? *[An aphid]*

   • The ladybug lands on the leaf and begins to crawl.

   • She crawls under the leaf and carefully lays her eggs.

3. Show the children the yellow egg and glue it (or draw an egg) onto the leaf on the same side as your name.

## Laying Ladybug Eggs

1. Have each child go to the work table and find the leaf with his or her name on it.

2. "Fly" the paper ladybug to the children's leaves and pretend she is laying an egg on each child's leaf. (If you have paper eggs, distribute them on the leaves.)

3. Have the children glue or draw the eggs onto their leaves.

4. Ask, "What do you think will hatch out of the eggs?"

*Session 2*

# BABY LADYBUGS

## Choices For Making Baby Ladybugs

Making baby ladybugs helps the children remember what ladybug larvae look like. The boys and girls can use the baby ladybugs in their dramas and pretend they are hatching from eggs and eating aphids.

The children can design and cut out their own baby ladybugs or they can use the paper cutouts. If they use the cutouts, read the Getting Ready and Making Baby Ladybugs sections that follow.

## WHAT YOU NEED

### For the whole group

➤ 1 pair of scissors
➤ 1 tray
➤ Newspaper, enough to cover the tray and work tables
➤ 1 Ladybug, Eggs, and Baby Ladybugs poster
➤ Pictures of ladybug eggs and larvae  (See Resource Books on page 75 for books with colored pictures of eggs and larvae.)
➤ Live ladybug eggs and larvae on leaves

> ➤ *Ladybug eggs and larvae are difficult to find, but having a few for the children to observe is well worth the time it takes to look for them. Search in the area where the children released their ladybugs. Also look on plants that attract aphids, such as rose bushes, dandelions, nasturtiums, pea, tomato, bean, and strawberry plants.*

### For each child and yourself

➤ 1 paper ladybug
➤ 1 paper leaf with an egg and an aphid
➤ 1 sheet of 2" x 4" orange construction paper  (Include an extra one for the drama.)
➤ 1 sheet of 1½" x 2" black construction paper  (Include an extra one for the drama.)
➤ 1 black crayon or marker
➤ 1 container of white paste or glue

# GETTING READY

## Anytime Before the Activity

1. You need a paper ladybug larva for the drama, each child, and yourself. Use the patterns on page 50 to cut out the larvae and legs.

   - Use the orange paper to cut out the larvae (pattern G).

   - Use the black paper to cut out six legs (pattern J) for each larva.

2. Follow the instructions on page 48 to make a larva for the drama.

3. Write each child's name on a larva cutout, or have the children write their own names during the activity.

4. To care for live ladybug larvae, follow the instructions on the care of adult ladybugs. (See pages 14-15.)

➢ *One teacher copied the larva and pupa patterns onto orange paper for the children to cut out.*

## Immediately Before the Activity

1. Place one larva cutout, six legs, one black crayon, paste, and newspaper on a tray. Put the tray in the area where you present the activities.

2. Spread newspaper on the tables and place one baby ladybug cutout, six legs, one black crayon, and paste at each child's work place.

3. Have one paper larva and one paper leaf with an egg and one or more aphids in the area where you present the drama.

## Introducing Baby Ladybugs

1. Ask, "What do you think baby ladybugs look like?" Encourage the children to use their imaginations, and accept all answers.

2. Show the Ladybug, Eggs, and Baby Ladybugs poster. Have a child find the tiny animal that is crawling out of the egg. Tell the children that this little animal is a baby ladybug. Have another child find a bigger baby ladybug. Ask, "What colors do you see on the bigger baby ladybug?"

3. If you were able to find live ladybug eggs and larvae, let the children search for them on the leaves. If you were unable to find them, show the color photographs and drawings of ladybug eggs and larvae. Keep the ladybug books in the room so that the children can look at them as often as they like.

4. Encourage the youngsters to describe the colors of the leaves, eggs, and baby ladybugs.

5. Take the group outside to look on and under leaves for live adult ladybugs, tiny eggs, and baby ladybugs. They also can look for birds that may eat ladybugs.

## Baby Ladybug Drama

1. Back inside in the circle, hide the paper egg and larva under the paper leaf. Place one or more aphids on top of the leaf.

2. Use the leaf, aphid(s), and larva to present another short drama.

   • After many days, the eggs hatch and baby ladybugs crawl out. (Crawl the larva from under the leaf, and over to an aphid.)

   • The baby ladybug eats all the aphids it can catch, and grows bigger.

## Making Baby Ladybugs

1. Along with the children, count the six legs on the larva used in the drama.

2. Ask, "What colors do you see on the baby ladybug?" *[Orange, Black]*

3. Have the children help you make a ladybug larva.

   • Ask, "How many legs does the baby ladybug have?" *[Six]* Glue six legs onto the paper larva cutout.

   • Ask, "What does the baby ladybug have on its face?" *[Eyes, Mouth]* Draw two eyes and a mouth.

   • Ask, "What does the baby ladybug have on its back?" *[Spots, Stripes]* Draw spots and stripes on the larva with a black crayon.

4. Have the children go to the work tables and make their own larvae.

## Creative Play

1. Allow time for the children to play freely with their own leaves, eggs, aphids, baby ladybugs, and adult ladybugs.

2. If you plan to do Activity 4: Ladybug Pupae and Life Cycle, tell the children to leave their projects in the room because they will make something new to live on their leaves.

## Role Playing

1. Along with the children, role-play the first two stages in the life cycle of the ladybug. Pretend to be:

   • An egg. (Curl up in a squatting position.)
   • A little baby ladybug crawling out of the egg and over to an aphid, then eating aphids and growing bigger. (Crawl. Then pretend to eat and stretch out.)

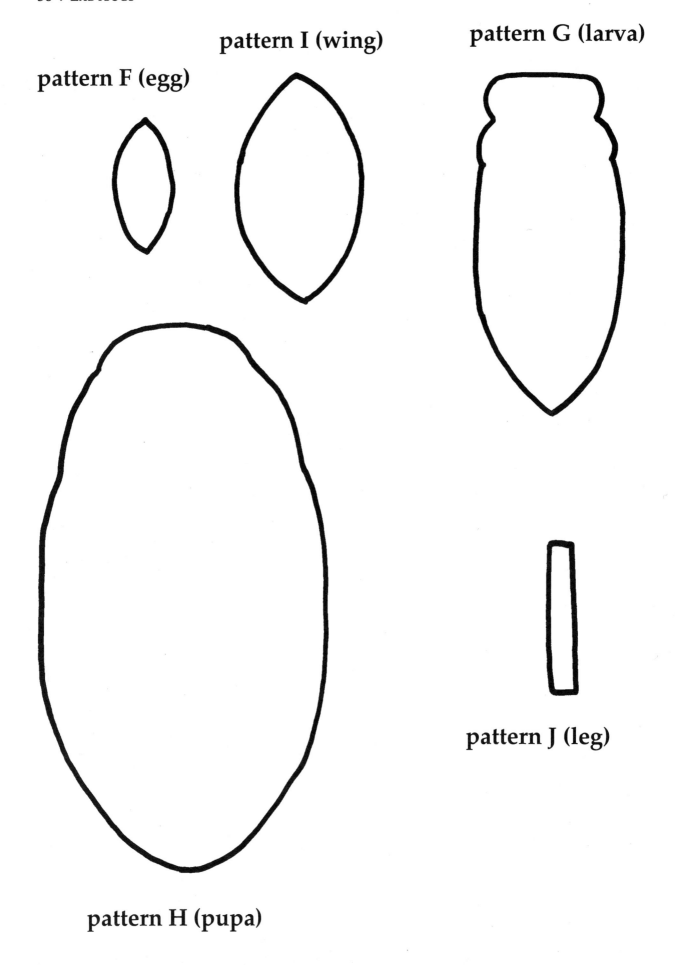

pattern F (egg)

pattern I (wing)

pattern G (larva)

pattern H (pupa)

pattern J (leg)

# LADYBUG EGGS AND BABY LADYBUGS

*— Activity 4 —*

# LADYBUG PUPAE AND LIFE CYCLE

## Overview

As the children observe live ladybug pupae and look at pictures of pupae, they discover that ladybug babies change into pupae before becoming adults. While watching a short drama and making paper pupae, the youngsters learn that the pupae stay very still and develop wings, but cannot fly.

The children review the life cycle of the ladybug by participating in a drama, pointing out the larva and pupa on a poster, and role-playing the ladybug life cycle, which are fun ways to recall the changes from egg to adult.

## Choices For Presenting Activity 4

The changes that occur during the ladybug's life cycle may be difficult for preschoolers to understand, especially the idea of change during the pupal stage. Therefore, you may decide not to do this chapter with three-and four-year-olds. Without discussing the specific stages in the ladybug life cycle, you can tell preschoolers that ladybug babies grow bigger and change into grown-up ladybugs.

*Session 1*

## LADYBUG PUPAE

## Choices For Making Ladybug Pupae

There is an advantage to each child having a paper egg, larva, pupa, and ladybug. They can make up their own life cycle dramas and arrange their own eggs, larvae, pupae, and ladybugs in order of development.

The children can design and cut out their own pupae or they can use the paper cutouts to make their pupae. If they use the cutouts, read the Getting Ready and Making Ladybug Pupae sections that follow.

## WHAT YOU NEED

### For the whole group

➤ 1 tray
➤ Newspaper, enough to cover the tray and work tables
➤ Live ladybug eggs, larvae, and pupae on leaves
➤ Pictures of ladybug pupae (See Resource Books on page 75 for books with colored pictures of pupae.)
➤ 1 Larvae and Pupa poster

### For each child and yourself

➤ 1 paper ladybug
➤ 1 paper leaf with an egg and aphid
➤ 1 paper larva
➤ 1 sheet of 4½" x 6" orange construction paper (Include an extra one for the drama.)
➤ 1 sheet of 1½" x 2" black construction paper (Include an extra one for the drama.)
➤ 1 black crayon or marker
➤ 1 container of white paste or glue
➤ 1 pair of scissors

## GETTING READY

### Anytime Before the Activity

1. You need one paper ladybug pupa for the drama, for each child, and for yourself. Use the patterns on page 50 to cut out the pupae, wings, and legs.

   • Use the orange paper to cut out one pupa (pattern H) and two wings (pattern I) for each pupa.

   • Use the black paper to cut out six legs (pattern J) for each pupa.

2. Follow the instructions on page 56 to make a pupa for the drama.

3. Write each child's name on a pupa cutout, or have the children write their own names on their cutout during the activity.

### Immediately Before the Activity

1. Place one pupa cutout, six legs, two wings, one black crayon, paste, and newspaper on a tray. Put the tray in the area where you present the activities.

➤ *Some teachers have their students add wings to their paper larvae to turn them into pupae.*

2. Spread newspaper on the tables and place one pupa cutout, six legs, two wings, one black crayon, and paste at each child's work place.

## Introducing Pupae

1. Encourage the children to look at the live larvae and pupae. If you were unable to find them, show the colored photographs or drawings of larvae and pupae in the ladybug books. Keep the books in the room so that the children can look at them as often as they like.

2. When a child discovers a pupa, or when you point one out in a picture, ask, "What do you think this is?"

3. Tell the group that it is a ladybug that is changing from a baby ladybug to a grown-up ladybug. It is called a *pupa.*

4. Show the Larvae and Pupa poster. Have a child find the pupa. Have another child find the two larvae.

5. Ask, "How is the pupa different from the baby ladybug?" *[It has wings]*

## Pupae Drama

1. Back in the circle, hide the paper pupa under the paper leaf. Have the larva and aphid on the leaf.

2. Use the leaf, aphid, larva, and pupa to present a short drama.

   • The baby ladybug eats all the aphids it can catch, and grows bigger.

   • One day the baby ladybug crawls under the leaf and stays very still. (Hide the larva under the leaf, between the pupa and the leaf.)

   • Something exciting happens.

   • The baby ladybug is changing into a grown-up ladybug. Now it is called a *pupa.* (Turn the leaf over so that you see only the pupa. The larva is still hidden under the pupa.)

   • What does the pupa have? *[Legs, Eyes, Wings]* The little wings stay very still. The pupa cannot move its wings.

## Making Ladybug Pupae

1. Along with the children, count the legs on the pupa used in the drama.

2. Ask, "What colors do you see on the pupa?" *[Orange and black]*

3. Have the children help you make a ladybug pupa.
   - Glue six legs onto the paper pupa cutout.
   - Draw two eyes.
   - Use a black crayon to decorate the pupa.
   - Ask, "What does the pupa have that the baby ladybug doesn't have?" *[Wings]* Glue wings onto the pupa.

2. Give a pupa cutout to each child.

3. Have the children make their own pupae.

## Creative Play

Allow time for the children to play freely with their leaves, eggs, aphids, larvae, pupae, and adult ladybugs.

## Comparing

1. When a child shows you his or her ladybug, larva, and pupa, ask a few comparison questions, such as
   - How is the grown-up ladybug different from the little baby ladybug? *[It's bigger. It's red. It has four wings and two feelers]*
   - How is the pupa the same as the grown-up ladybug? *[It has legs and wings]*

2. Have the children look again at the living eggs, larvae, and pupae. Encourage them to describe what they see.

## Role Playing

1. Ask, "How would you pretend to be a pupa?"

2. Use the children's suggestions to role-play the pupal stage of the ladybug's life cycle.

3. If the children don't have any suggestions, then stay very still. Make wings by folding your arms and holding them close to your chest. Encourage the youngsters to role play with you.

*Session 2*

# THE LADYBUG LIFE CYCLE

## WHAT YOU NEED

### For the whole group

➤ 1 Ladybug, Eggs, Larvae, and Pupa poster

### For each child and yourself

➤ 1 paper ladybug
➤ 1 paper leaf with an aphid and egg
➤ 1 paper larva
➤ 1 paper pupa

## GETTING READY

1. Color the Ladybug, Eggs, Larvae, and Pupa poster. Color the leaf green, the eggs yellow, the ladybug red, and the larvae and pupae orange.

2. Practice the drama before beginning the Life Cycle Drama.

## Ladybug Life Cycle Poster

1. Show the group the Ladybug, Eggs, Larvae, and Pupa poster.

2. Ask, "What do you think the ladybug is doing?" *[Laying eggs]*

3. Ask a child to point to an egg and to the tiny animal that is crawling out of the egg.

4. Ask, "What do you think this animal is?" *[A baby ladybug, or larva]*

5. Tell a child to point to a baby ladybug that has grown bigger. Ask, "What do you see on the baby ladybug?" *[Head, Eyes, Legs]*

6. Along with the children, count the larva's legs. Ask, "Does the baby ladybug have any wings?" *[No]*

> ➤ *Some teachers talk about and show pictures of a child's growth from a newborn baby to an adult before presenting the life cycle of the ladybug.*

> ➤ *One teacher laminated several paper ladybug eggs, larvae, and pupae for the children to use in the classroom after they took their projects home.*

7. Show the children the pupa.

8. Tell the group that this ladybug is changing from a baby lady-bug to a grown-up ladybug. It has little wings but it cannot fly. Ask, "What is it called?" *[A pupa]*

9. Ask a child to find the little wings on the pupa.

10. Hang the poster in the room for the children to look at.

## Life Cycle Drama in Review

1. Use the paper ladybug, leaf with an aphid, larva, and pupa to present a drama showing the changes that occur during a ladybug's life cycle. Hide the larva and pupa under the leaf. Place the aphid on top of the leaf.

2. Tell the following story as you act out the drama.

   • A mother ladybug flies in the sky looking for an aphid on a leaf. Do you see an aphid? (Ask a child to point to the aphid.)

   • The mother is about to lay her eggs. She wants her babies to have something to eat when they crawl out of their eggs. What could a baby ladybug eat on this leaf? *[An aphid]*

   • The ladybug lands on the leaf and begins to crawl.

   • She crawls under the leaf and carefully lays her eggs.

   • After many days, the eggs hatch and baby ladybugs crawl out. (Crawl the larva from under the leaf, and over to the aphid.)

   • The baby ladybug eats all the aphids it can catch, and grows bigger.

   • One day the baby ladybug crawls under the leaf and stays very still. (Hide the larva under the leaf, between the pupa and the leaf.)

   • The baby begins to change. What does the baby ladybug change into? (Turn the leaf over so that you see only the pupa. The larva is still hidden under the pupa.)

   • What does the pupa have now? *[Wings]* The little wings stay very still. The pupa cannot move its wings.

   • The pupa continues to change until it becomes a grown-up ladybug. (Turn the leaf over to hide the pupa. Put the ladybug on the leaf.)

- The ladybug stands on the leaf. She moves her big wings up and down.
- What do you think the grown-up ladybug can do that the pupa can't do? [Fly]
- Off she flies into the blue sky.

## From Egg to Adult

1. Randomly place on the floor a paper leaf with an egg, a larva, a pupa, and an adult ladybug.

2. Have the children help you arrange them in a straight line in order from egg to adult (egg, larva, pupa, and adult).

   - Ask, "Which one crawled out of the egg?" [Larva]
   - Have a child place the larva next to the egg.
   - Say, "The little baby ladybug ate aphids and grew bigger. It began to change. Then what did it look like?" [A Pupa]
   - Have a child place the pupa next to the larva.
   - Say, "The pupa stayed very still and changed. What did it change into?" [A Ladybug]
   - Have a child place the adult ladybug next to the pupa.
   - Ask, "What did the grown-up ladybug do?" [Fly away]

2. Encourage the children to put their paper eggs, larvae, pupae, and adult ladybugs in order of development.

➤ *One teacher played background music while the children role play the ladybug life cycle.*

### Role Playing

1. Along with the children, role-play the complete life cycle of the ladybug. Pretend to be:

   • An egg. (Curl up in a squatting position.)

   • A larva crawling out of the egg and over to an aphid, then eating aphids and growing bigger. (Crawl. Pretend to eat and stretch out.)

   • A pupa. (Be still. Make wings by folding your arms and holding them close to your chest.)

   • An adult. (Pretend to fly away, or "fly" outside to look for aphids. You may want to tie the paper wings on the children.)

2. Encourage the children to pretend they are saving the plants in the yard by eating all the aphids.

## GOING FURTHER

1. Have each child make a Ladybug Life Cycle Book. Copy an egg, larva, pupa, and ladybug drawing on page 61 for each child or let the children draw their own. They can write or dictate stories to add to the books.

2. Use the egg, larva, pupa, and ladybug drawings to create cards that the children can arrange in a straight line in order from egg to adult.

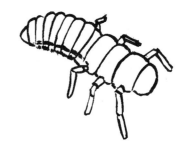

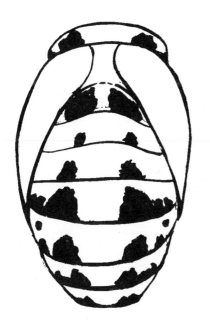

# LARVAE AND PUPA

# LADYBUG, EGGS, LARVAE, AND PUPA

*— Activity 5 —*

# LADYBUGS RESCUE THE ORANGE TREES

## Overview

The group watches a short drama about how ladybugs once saved the orange trees in California. The children learn that ladybugs eat tiny animals called scale, which can destroy orange trees. The children eat orange slices and thank the ladybugs for the oranges. They review the major concepts introduced in this unit, such as ladybug defenses, life cycle, and the foods ladybugs eat.

## *Session 1*

# LADYBUGS, SCALE, AND ORANGES

## WHAT YOU NEED

### For the whole group

- ➤ 1 Scale on a Branch poster
- ➤ 3 paper ladybugs from Activity 1: Getting to Know Ladybugs on page 13
- ➤ 1 larva from Activity 3: Eggs and Baby Ladybugs on page 43
- ➤ 1 pupa from Activity 4: Ladybug Pupae and Life Cycle on page 53
- ➤ 6 sheets of 8" x 8" orange construction paper
- ➤ 1 sheet of 12" x 18" brown paper
- ➤ 3 sheets of 9" x 12" green construction paper
- ➤ 1 sheet of 24" x 30" blue paper or poster board
- ➤ 5 white peel-and-stick dots
- ➤ 1 container of white glue
- ➤ 1 roll of tape
- ➤ 1 brown crayon

**Optional**
➤ 1 clear plastic container with a lid
➤ 1 branch from an orange tree with ripe oranges
➤ 1 or more branches with live scale (Live scale are difficult to find, but having some for the children to observe is well worth the time it takes to look for them. Look on a variety of trees, including citrus, fig, pine, hibiscus, and elm trees. See page 74 for more information on scale.)
➤ Live ladybugs

## For each child and yourself

➤ 1 orange slice

# GETTING READY

## Anytime Before the Activity

1. Make a branch mural. (See the drawing on this page.)

   a. Cut the brown sheet of paper into two 6" x 18" rectangles.

   b. Tape or glue the two short ends together to make the branch.

   c. Tape or glue the branch to the blue paper.

   d. Cut the corners off the three sheets of green paper to make leaves.

   e. Tape or glue these leaves onto the branch.

   f. Use the sheets of orange paper to cut out six large oranges for the mural.

   g. Tape only three oranges onto the branch.

   h. Stick or draw the "scale" onto the leaves and branch.

2. Color the poster. Make the leaf brown so it looks dead, and leave the scale white.

## Immediately Before the Activity

1. Place the branch mural on the floor in an area where the children can sit in front of it.

2. Have the three paper oranges, three adult ladybugs, one larva, and one pupa near the mural.

## Observing Scale

1. Gather the children in a circle on the floor, and show them the Scale on a Branch poster. Explain that scale are small insects.

**Note:** The scale insects on the poster are Cottony-Cushion Scale, the insects that damaged the orange trees in California.

2. Ask, "What do you think the scale are doing to this plant?" *[Sucking juices from it]* Tell the children that scale can suck all the juices from the leaves and stems. The plant gets sick and may die.

3. Ask, "Do you think the leaf is healthy?" *[No]* "Why?" *[Because it's brown]*

### Optional

1. Let the children find live scale on a branch or on leaves. If the scale looks different from the kind in the poster, tell the children that there are many different kinds of scale.

2. Encourage them to touch the scale and describe them. Ask, "What does the scale feel like?"

3. Put a leaf with scale on it and ladybugs in a clear plastic jar with a lid. Encourage the children to watch and see if the ladybugs eat the scale.

4. Ask, "How do ladybugs help plants?" *[They eat the scale that hurt the plants]*

### Optional: Observing an Orange Branch

1. Place the orange branch in an area where a group of children can gather around it.

2. Encourage the youngsters to touch and smell the oranges and the leaves.

3. Have them compare the texture on the oranges with the leaves.

## How Ladybugs Helped the Orange Trees

1. Gather the children in front of the mural.

2. Tell the group a story about how ladybugs once saved the orange trees in California. Act out the drama as you tell the story.

   - A long, long time ago all the orange trees in California were dying. The farmers were worried because they wouldn't have enough oranges to sell to all the people who love to eat oranges.

   - One day a farmer noticed some very tiny, white animals on his orange trees. (Point to the white dots.) What do you think the tiny, white animals were? *[Scale]* The scale were sucking juices from the orange trees and making the trees die.

   - The farmer wanted to get rid of the scale. What do you think the farmer decided to do? (If the children don't suggest getting ladybugs ask, "What animal eats scale?")

   - He got a lot of ladybugs and put them on his orange trees to eat the scale. (Place several paper ladybugs on the branch.)

   - The ladybugs ate and ate. (Peel three dots off the branch.)

   - They had babies that ate and ate. (Place the ladybug babies on a leaf and peel off the rest of the dots.)

   - After a long time, the farmer couldn't find any scale on his orange trees.

   - The trees became healthy again. A lot of oranges grew on the trees. (Place three more oranges on the tree.)

   - The ladybugs saved the orange trees. Some farmers still use ladybugs to eat scale so that the orange trees stay healthy, and we stay healthy too because we have plenty of oranges to eat and orange juice to drink.

## Eating Oranges

1. As you distribute orange slices for the children to eat ask, "How did the ladybugs help the orange trees?" *[They ate the scale that were killing the trees]*

2. Have the group thank the ladybugs for the oranges.

*Session 2*

# REVIEWING

## WHAT YOU NEED

### For the whole group

➤ 1 branch mural
    from Session 1:  Ladybugs, Scale, and Oranges on page  66
➤ 1 or more paper ladybugs
    from Activity 1:  Getting to Know Ladybugs on page 13
➤ 1 larva
    from Activity 3:  Eggs and Baby Ladybugs on page 43
➤ 1 pupa
    from Activity 4:  Ladybug Pupae and Life Cycle on page 53
➤ 1 paper leaf with an egg and aphid

### Reviewing

1. Tell a story and present a short drama about ladybugs, their defenses, life cycle, and the foods they eat.  Use the "bird" (your hand) and some of the paper projects (ladybugs, leaves, eggs, larvae, pupae, aphids, and oranges with scale) to act out the story.

2. After the story, ask

   • What do birds eat?  *[Ladybugs]* Have the "bird" pick up a ladybug.

   • What do ladybugs eat?  *[Aphids and scale]* Pretend a ladybug is eating aphids and scale.

   • What do aphids and scale eat? *[Juices from plants]*

   • What do you think would happen if birds ate all the ladybugs in the world?

## GOING FURTHER

1. Let the children design their own oranges with stems, leaves, and scale. They can make them out of colored construction paper to use in creative-play activities, or they can paint them.

2. To assess how much the children learned about the body structure of a ladybug, put out paint, brushes, and paper so that each child can paint a ladybug. Compare these paintings with the ones the children did at the beginning of the unit.

3. Have the children work in groups to make a large ladybug mural. They can paint a colorful tree with ladybugs, aphids, larvae, pupae, birds, oranges, and scale.

4. Let the children take their projects home and encourage them to share the projects, the dramas, and everything they learned about ladybugs with their families and friends.

# SCALE ON A BRANCH

# BACKGROUND INFORMATION

## Variety of Ladybugs

Ladybugs, also known as Ladybirds and Ladybird Beetles, are attractive because of their colorful spotted design. People usually think of them as red with black spots, but ladybugs can be a variety of colors. They can be yellow with black spots; orange with yellow spots; or black or brown with white, red, or yellow spots. Some have no spots.

The names of ladybugs often reflect the number of spots on the cover wings. There is the very common two-spot ladybug, the ten-spot, seven-spot, fourteen-spot, and others. There are more than 4,000 varieties of ladybugs in the world and about 400 in the United States.

## Body Structure

Like other insects, ladybugs have three body sections (head, thorax, and abdomen), six legs, and two antennae. The legs are attached to the thorax, the middle section. However, on the ladybug, the three body sections are not obvious and the legs often look as though they are attached to the abdomen.

Ladybugs have two large transparent flying wings, which they tuck under their pair of cover wings when they are not in flight. The cover wings are hard, shell-like, and provide protection for the ladybug. Two sharp claws and sticky pads at the end of each leg help the ladybug to climb on slippery surfaces.

## Life Cycle

Female ladybugs lay yellow or orange eggs in small clusters on stems and under the leaves of plants that are infested with aphids, scale, and other plant-eating insects. After several days, the eggs hatch into larvae, which are about a third of an inch long and covered with sharp hairlike structures called bristles. The larvae eat the tiny insects on the plants and grow rapidly.

When a larva is full grown, it attaches its rear end to a leaf or branch with a sticky substance that resembles a silky pad. It then enters the pupal stage, which lasts from five to seven days. During this stage, a head, legs, and small cover wings become visible as the pupa changes into an adult ladybug. The pupal skin splits open and a pale-colored ladybug emerges. The insect dries its wings and can fly within an hour. Within several hours after the adult emerges, spots appear and the skin changes to its final color. This dramatic change, or metamorphosis, from egg to adult takes about one month. Ladybugs live for about one year.

For books with information on the ladybug life cycle and color photographs and illustrations of ladybug eggs, larvae, and pupae, see Resource Books on page 75.

## Ladybug Defenses

Ladybugs have numerous defenses. When danger is near, they flop on their backs and stay very still until it is safe for them to walk or fly away. They produce a vile-tasting and bad-smelling fluid from their joints that keeps some animals from eating them. Like many other animals, their bright colors warn predators of the bad taste. Ladybugs may bite if squeezed. As protection against cold weather, they cluster in large groups in cracks, hollow logs, under bark, and under fallen leaves.

## An Alternative to Insecticides

Adult ladybugs, as well as ladybug larvae, eat huge quantities of plant-eating insects. In several countries, including the United States, ladybugs are raised and sold to control insect pests. Unfortunately, insecticides are used more widely than ladybugs to kill insects. While feeding on these pests, ladybugs become the victims of insecticides and seem more vulnerable to these poisonous chemicals than do aphids, scale, and some other plant-eating insects. Increasing the number of ladybugs and other natural enemies of plant-eating insects to control damage is a wise alternative to insecticides.

## Aphids

Aphids, also called plant lice, are tiny pear-shaped insects. They come in many colors: green, brown, black, purple, yellow, or orange. Most aphids are wingless, but some have wings. When winged aphids rest, they usually hold their wings vertically above their bodies.

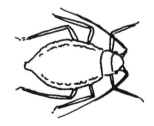

Aphids are often found clustered at the tips of young plants and also at the growing tips of older plants where the leaves are soft. Some of the plants that attract aphids include rose bushes, dandelions, nasturtiums, pea, bean, tomato, and strawberry plants. Aphids have a strawlike mouthpiece, called a proboscis, which they use to suck the sap from leaves, stems, and branches. Their feeding can cause plants to wilt and die. Aphids also carry plant diseases. When aphids eat too much, they excrete the excess from the tips of their abdomens in a sweet liquid called honeydew. Ants and other insects eat the honey dew.

Aphids have many enemies. They are eaten by insects, especially ladybug larvae, and some birds. Insecticides kill large numbers of aphids.

## Scale

Scale are a large group of sucking insects closely related to aphids. Like aphids, they have a proboscis, which they use to suck sap from leaves and branches.

Scale come in a variety of sizes, shapes, and colors. The largest are about one inch long, but most are smaller. Cottony-cushion scale are white or tan, while adult terrapin scale are brown and resemble tiny turtle shells. Mealy bugs are a white scale. A secretion of wax or resin, which is usually mealy or cottony, covers all scale insects. Many have a scale-like covering.

One female scale may produce as many as 30 million young in one year. Some scale insects lay eggs and some give birth to living young. The eggs are laid under the female's body, or under cottony or mealy secretions. The larvae are flat, active, oval-shaped, and difficult to see. They have six legs and two antennae at first but quickly lose them.

As adults, female scale are wingless and many lack legs and eyes. Some adult males are wingless, and some have a single pair of wings. These winged males resemble gnats. All males lack mouthparts and do not eat.

Scale live in large colonies, which can cover and destroy plants. They can infest a variety of trees and shrubs, including citrus, pine, hibiscus, elm, banana, fig, heath, and many more. Scale are very difficult to control. Ladybugs and some types of small wasps help farmers and gardeners by eating huge numbers of these pests.

Even though scale are destructive to plants, scientists have discovered beneficial uses for the secretions that some scale produce. Shellacs, polishes, buttons, linoleum, and many other products contain natural substances made by scale.

Cottony-Cushion Scale

Terrapin Scale

Mealy Bug or White Scale

# RESOURCE BOOKS

These books have information on the ladybug life cycle and color illustrations or photographs of ladybugs, eggs, larvae, pupae, and aphids.

**Ladybirds**
by Althea Braithwaite
Longman Group, Essex, U.K.  1985

**Ladybug**
by Barrie Watts
Silver Burdett Press,
Morristown, New Jersey. 1987

**The Ladybug and Other Insects**
by Gallimard Jeunese and Pascale de Bourgoing
Scholastic, New York. 1991

**Ladybugs**
by Silvia Johnson
Lerner Publications, Minneapolis. 1983

**Life of the Ladybug**
by A. and H. Fischer-Nagel
Carolrhoda Books, Minneapolis. 1981
*Out of print*

# RESOURCE MATERIALS

You probably can obtain live ladybugs from your local nursery, or they can order them for you. You can also order your own from:

Insect Lore Products (Sells and ships live ladybugs.)
P.O. Box 1535
132 S. Beech, Shafter, CA 93263

Orders Only:  1-800-LIVE BUG
Customer Service:  1-805-746-6047

# LITERATURE CONNECTIONS

➤ *You may wish to examine the literature listings for the GEMS teacher's guides* Animal Defenses, Buzzing A Hive, Hide A Butterfly, *and* Terrarium Habitats *in the GEMS handbook* Once Upon A GEMS Guide: Connecting Young People's Literature to Great Explorations in Math and Science. *Also, please see the age-appropriate listings in the science themes—especially Patterns of Change and Diversity & Unity—as well as the math strands sections in the handbook.*

*In addition, the four teacher's guides include exciting activities that would make excellent accompaniments to Ladybugs.*

**Flit, Flutter, Fly!**
**Poems About Bugs and Other Crawly Creatures**
selected by Lee Bennett Hopkins; illustrated by Peter Palagonia
Doubleday, New York. 1992

These poems, by a variety of authors, are about insects and other creatures that crawl, including ones about ladybugs. The verses are gentle and the illustrations soothing—a good combination for young children.

**The Grouchy Ladybug**
by Eric Carle
Harper and Row, New York. 1986

The grouchy ladybug and the friendly ladybug want to eat all the aphids on a leaf. The grouchy ladybug challenges the friendly ladybug to a fight, and then challenges every other animal it meets regardless of the animal's size or strength. This book is a wonderful springboard to measurement activities involving size for young children. There is a clock on each page to chronicle the day in hours for older children. While this book can be read anytime when presenting *Ladybugs*, it works especially well in Activity 2, Session 1.

**Ladybug, Ladybug**
by Ruth Brown
E.P. Dutton, New York. 1988

Based on the nursery rhyme "Ladybug, Ladybug, Fly Away Home," this beautifully illustrated story captures a ladybug's flight home, where she finds her children safely sleeping. While this book can be read anytime when presenting *Ladybugs*, it works especially well in Activity 1, Session 1.

# GLOSSARY

**Antennae** (an-TEN-nee): A pair of long, sensitive feelers that insects use to touch, taste, and smell.

**Larva, larvae** (LAR-vee): An immature form of an animal that is structurally unlike the adult.

**Metamorphosis** (MET-ah-MORE-fo-siss): The complete and dramatic change of form an animal undergoes to become an adult.

**Proboscis** (pro-BOS-kiss) or (pro-BOS-sis): A straw-like mouthpiece that insects use to suck nectar or sap from plants.

**Pupa** (PEW-pah), **pupae** (PEW-pee): The stage between a larva and adult in the metamorphosis of some insects.

# SUMMARY OUTLINES

## ACTIVITY 1: GETTING TO KNOW LADYBUGS

### Session 1: Introducing Ladybugs

**Observing Live Ladybugs**
1. Begin with: "I'm thinking of a very tiny animal that's red with black spots."
2. Give each child a ladybug in container. Ask questions to encourage observation. Afterward, collect containers.

**Observing the Ladybug Poster**
1. Display poster. Children talk about experiences with ladybugs.
2. Have group count legs, eyes, feelers (*antennae*) with you.
3. Ask what children use to touch and smell—what about ladybugs?
   [*feelers*]

**Observing the Flying Ladybug Poster**
1. Display poster. Children guess what ladybug is doing.
2. Explain kinds of wings: *cover wings*, *flying wings*; have children count.

**Ladybug Pictures, Ladybug Hunt, Role Play**
1. Have books for children with photos and drawings.
2. Take children outside to look for ladybugs.
3. Children pretend to be flying/crawling ladybugs.

**Letting Live Ladybugs Fly Away**
1. While still outside, give each child a ladybug in container.
2. Encourage children to gently allow ladybugs to crawl on their hands.
3. As it may arise, explain ladybug use of "bad smells" for protection.
4. As ladybugs fly away, children count both types of wings.
*Note*: Keep/recapture at least three ladybugs with six or fewer spots.

### Session 2: Symmetry

**Symmetry and Me**
1. Ask for volunteer to demonstrate symmetry with yarn.
2. Point out eye on each side. What other parts of body are same on both sides? Introduce the word *symmetry* as appropriate.
3. Put yarn across waist and ask if body is same now on both sides.
4. Children work in pairs to observe symmetry in their bodies.
5. As appropriate look for symmetry in classroom objects.

**Symmetry Art Activities**
Consider doing some or all of the recommended art activities: Squish Paintings, Cutouts, Hole Punches.

**Ladybug Symmetry**
1. Ask if a ladybug's body is same on both sides.
2. Hand out Ladybug Spots sheet to each child to fold. Help as needed.
3. What things are same on both sides? What is the ladybug missing? [Spots]
4. Show children how to paint dots on one wing on one side. Count dots then fold. Ask how many dots will be on other wing. Accept

all guesses. Open and count!
5. Children make spots, count, fold sheet, then open it.
6. Look at live ladybugs/poster to see if number of spots same on both wings.

## Session 3: Making Paper Ladybugs

### Making Ladybug Models
1. Children help you make paper ladybug: write name, count parts, glue parts on, ask what is missing, then draw on eyes, mouth, spots.
2. Children make their own ladybugs.
3. Hand out flying and cover wings after legs are glued on.

## Session 4: Ladybug Defenses

### A Ladybug Enemy and Role-Playing Defenses
1. Explain that some birds eat ladybugs. Enact drama as in guide.
2. Take children outside on blanket they pretend is a branch.
3. Pretend to be a bird. Children fly away or roll off blanket, then lie still.
4. When all children are off blanket, hungry bird flies away.
5. In class, role play with paper ladybugs and black dot for bird's eye.

# ACTIVITY 2: LADYBUGS EATING APHIDS

## Session 1: Ladybugs, Plants, and Aphids

### Observing Live Aphids and Ladybugs
*Note*: If you don't have live aphids, show drawings or photos.
1. Show children live aphids, allow time for observation.
2. Aphids suck juices from plants. Look for brown spots. Are aphids there?
3. Pretend there is a garden: elicit suggestions for getting rid of aphids.
4. Put ladybugs, aphids, and leaves in containers. Have children observe. Ask: "What do aphids eat? What eats aphids? How do ladybugs help plants?"

### Observing the Poster and Nature
1. Show the Ladybugs Eating Aphids poster. Ask what is happening.
2. Have child count aphid's legs/feelers. What are feelers for? [smell and touch]
3. Go outside to look for aphids and ladybugs.

### Ladybugs Eating Aphid Popsicles
1. Children will pretend to be ladybugs, wear paper wings.
2. Show how to write names on and decorate their wings.
3. Tie wings on, go outside. Children fly around, looking for aphids.
4. Would they like to eat aphids? Bring out tray of "popsicle-aphids."
   *Optional*: Take aphid bodies off sticks for Making Paper Aphids activity.

## Session 2: Making Leaf Homes

### Making Paper Leaves
1. Have children make leaves bigger than their ladybugs.
2. Show how to snip corners or cut curves.
3. Be sure names are on leaves.

## Session 3: Making Aphids

### Making Paper Aphids
1. Show how to paste aphid abdomen onto body.
2. Ask number of legs, how it touches/feels, what it needs on its face.
3. Distribute paper bodies. Children make their own aphids.

### Creative Play
1. Give children their leaves, aphids, ladybugs.
2. Allow time for free play.

# ACTIVITY 3: EGGS AND BABY LADYBUGS

## Session 1: Ladybug Eggs

### Egg Laying Drama
1. Gather children in circle, with leaf, egg, aphid in middle.
2. Use these props with paper ladybug to present egg-laying drama.
3. Show children the egg and glue (or draw) it on leaf.

### Laying Ladybug Eggs
1. Have children find their leaves.
2. "Fly" paper ladybug to each leaf to lay eggs.
3. Have children glue (or draw) eggs on leaf. What will hatch?

## Session 2: Baby Ladybugs

### Introducing Baby Ladybugs
1. Ask what baby ladybugs look like. Accept all answers.
2. Show the Ladybug, Eggs, and Baby Ladybug poster.
3. Have children find animal emerging from egg, bigger ones, observe colors.
3. If you have live eggs/larvae children observe. If not, use photos/drawings.
4. Take children outside to look for ladybugs, eggs, babies, birds.

### Baby Ladybug Drama
1. Hide paper egg and larva under paper leaf, aphids on top.
2. Present drama of hatching eggs, babies crawling, eating aphids.

### Making Baby Ladybugs, Free Play, and Role Play
1. With children, count six legs on the larva.
2. Ask about colors on the baby ladybug.
3. Have children help you make a *larva*, then make their own.
4. Allow time for free play with leaves, eggs, aphids, baby and adult ladybugs.
5. Role play first two stages: (1) in egg (2) baby crawls from egg, eats aphids.

# ACTIVITY 4: LADYBUG PUPAE AND LIFE CYCLE

## Session 1: Ladybug Pupae

### Introducing Pupae
1. Look at live larvae and pupae, or at photos/drawings.
2. When child sees pupa, ask what it is. Explain it is a ladybug changing from a baby to a grown-up and is called a *pupa*.

3. Show Larvae and Pupa poster. Children find pupa and larvae. How does pupa differ from baby?

**Pupae Drama**

1. Hide paper pupa under paper leaf, with larva and aphid on top.
2. Present drama of baby eating aphids, growing, changing into pupa.

**Making Ladybug Pupae, Creative Play, Comparing, Role Playing**

1. Count legs, ask about colors, and have children help you make a ladybug pupa. What does the pupa have that the baby didn't? [*Wings*]
2. Give pupa cutout to each child and have them make their own.
3. Allow time for free play. Ask comparison questions.
4. Have children pretend to be pupae.

## Session 2: The Ladybug Life Cycle

**Ladybug Life Cycle Poster**

1. Show poster and ask what ladybug is doing. [*Laying eggs*]
2. Ask questions about life stages.

**Life Cycle Drama in Review/From Egg to Adult**

1. Act out drama that begins with ladybug laying eggs, as in guide.
2. Place paper leaf with egg, larva, pupa, and adult in random order on floor.
3. Have children help you arrange in order in a straight line.
4. Encourage children to do the same with their own.

**Role Playing**

1. Role-play complete life cycle as described in guide.
2. Encourage children to pretend they are saving plants by eating aphids.

# ACTIVITY 5: LADYBUGS RESCUE THE ORANGE TREES

## Session 1: Ladybugs, Scale, and Oranges

**Observing Scale**

1. Show children the Scale on a Branch poster. Discuss how *scale* harms plants.
   *Optional:* Observe live scale on branch/leaves and orange tree branch.

**How Ladybugs Helped the Orange Trees**

1. Tell true story of how ladybugs saved orange trees in California.
2. Act out drama as you tell story.

**Eating Oranges**

1. Give children orange slices to eat.
2. Ask how ladybugs helped orange trees. [*They ate scale that were killing the trees*]
2. Have the group thank ladybugs for the oranges.

## Session 2: Reviewing

1. Tell a story about ladybugs, their defenses, life cycle, foods. Use hand as a bird and bring some of the paper projects into the drama.
2. Ask questions about what birds, ladybugs, aphids, and scale eat. What if birds ate all ladybugs in the world?

# Assessment Suggestions

## Selected Student Outcomes

1. Students become familiar with ladybug structure and behavior as they observe and care for live ladybugs.

2. Students create models of ladybugs and enact their behaviors through dramatic play.

3. Students become familiar with the different life stages of a ladybug.

4. Students model predator-prey relationships through dramatic play.

5. Students gain an intuitive understanding of symmetry as they study the symmetrical external features of ladybug and human bodies.

## Built-In Assessment Activities

### Live Ladybugs in the Classroom

In Activity 1, Getting to Know Ladybugs, students observe live ladybugs and study their structure, symmetry, and behaviors. Through questions and discussions, the teacher can see how students describe and compare what they observed about ladybugs. (Outcome 1)

### Predict the Spots

In Activity 1, students paint a few spots on one half of a paper ladybug body. They then fold the body on the line of symmetry and predict how many spots will appear on the other half. Teacher can ask students to state their prediction and explain their reasoning. Through this process, students will demonstrate the degree to which they understand and can apply the concept of symmetry. (Outcome 5)

### Making Models and Role Playing

In Activity 2, Ladybugs Eating Aphids, students feed live aphids to their ladybugs. They pretend they are ladybugs as they eat aphid popsicles. They also draw an aphid on a leaf for their ladybug model to eat. During these activities, the teacher listens for descriptive language, detailed stories, explanations, and role plays. Student drawings and paper models can also be evaluated for detail and inclusion of body structures. (Outcomes 1, 2, 4)

### The Life Stages of a Ladybug

Activity 3, Eggs and Baby Ladybugs and Activity 4, Ladybug Pupae and Life Cycle introduce students to the life stages of the ladybug. They watch a drama of the life cycle and then make models of young ladybugs. The models are used to dramatize the ladybug life sequence. The teacher can observe how the students build the models, and enact the dramas and role plays. The teacher should watch for role plays (told in words or through dramatics) that use new vocabulary and concepts that relate to the ladybug life stages. Some students may be able to demonstrate the life cycle process.
(Outcome 2, 3)

# Additional Assessment Ideas

### Writing Ladybug Stories and Plays

Students can write or dictate stories about ladybugs and add illustrations. Teachers can assist students to create a play from their stories and perform it for classmates and families.
(Outcome 2, 3, 4)

### Ladybugs at Home

Send the ladybug projects home with a piece of paper. Ask families to help the student write down a story—by the student—that describes an aspect of ladybug life.
(Outcomes 2, 3, 4)

### More Creatures in the Classroom

Bring in other small creatures such as meal worms, earthworms, and pillbugs for your class to observe and care for. Have the students compare their structure, behavior, and life stages to those of the ladybug.
(Outcome 1)

### Symmetry Hunt

Have students find symmetrical objects in the classroom or at home. Students can draw pictures or dictate words to record their discoveries. Compile a class list of student responses.
(Outcome 5)

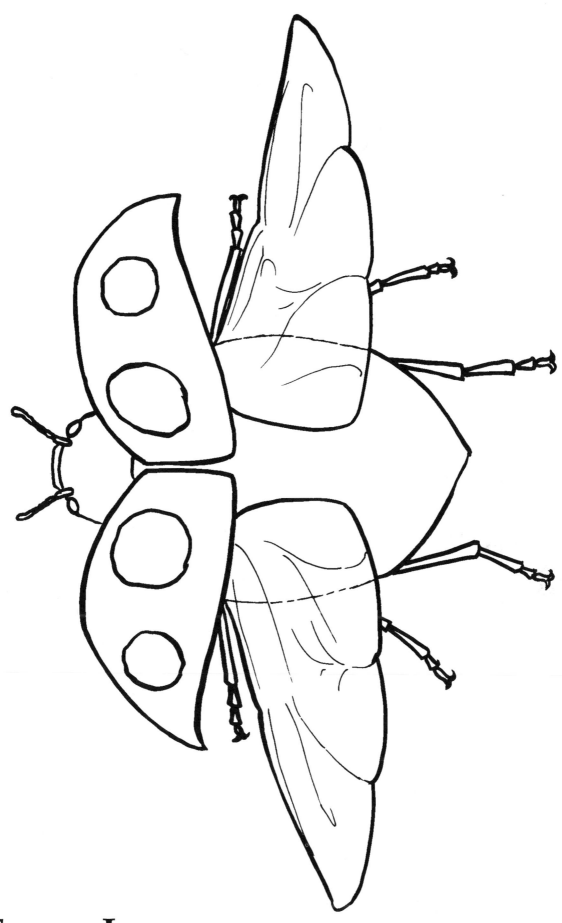

# FLYING LADYBUG

**May be duplicated for classroom use.**
© 1993 Regents of the University of California
LHS GEMS—*Ladybugs*

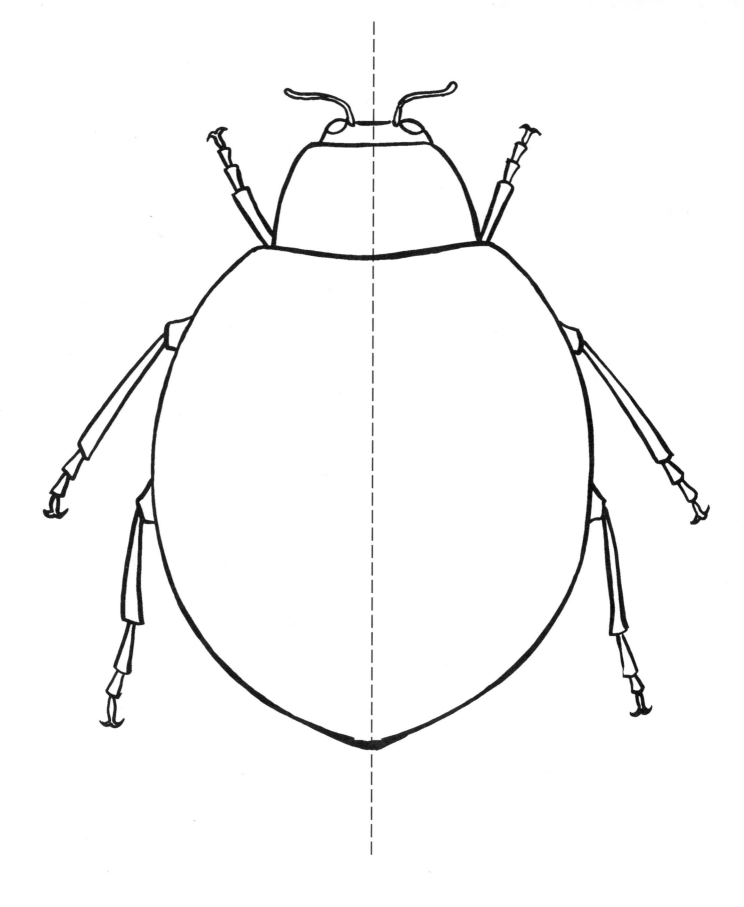

# Ladybug Spots

**May be duplicated for classroom use.**
© 1993 Regents of the University of California
LHS GEMS—*Ladybugs*

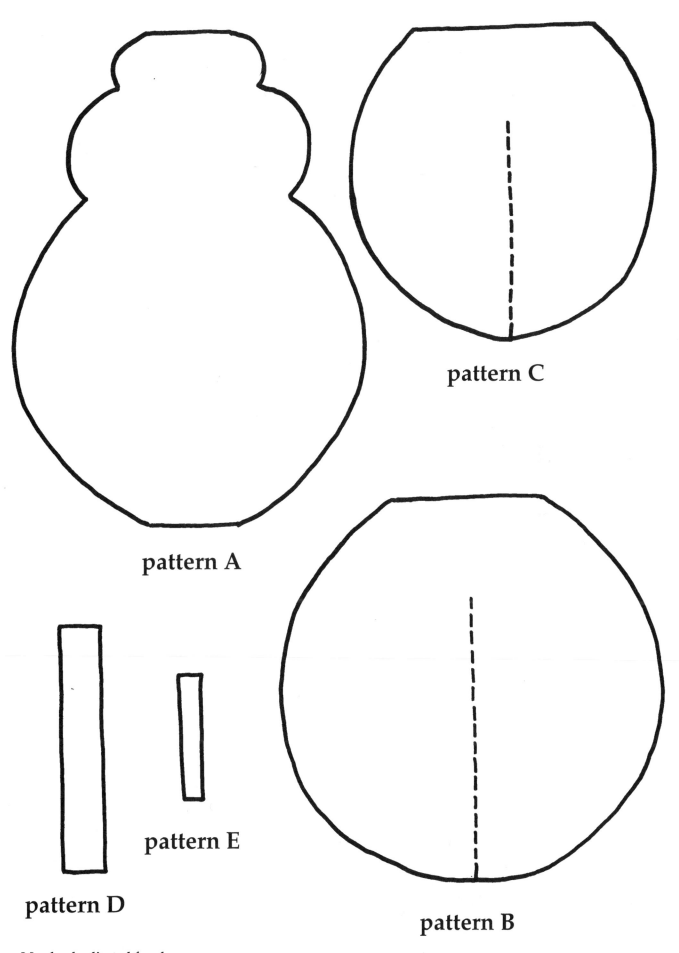

pattern C

pattern A

pattern E

pattern D

pattern B

**pattern K**

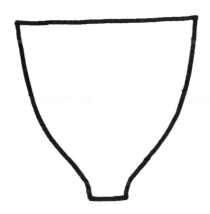

**pattern L**

# Aphid

**May be duplicated for classroom use.**
© 1993 Regents of the University of California
LHS GEMS—*Ladybugs*

pattern F (egg)

pattern I (wing)

pattern G (larva)

pattern H (pupa)

pattern J (leg)

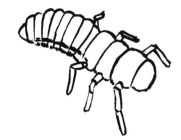

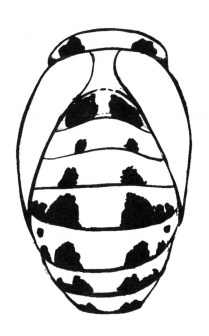

# Ladybug, Eggs, Larvae, and Pupa

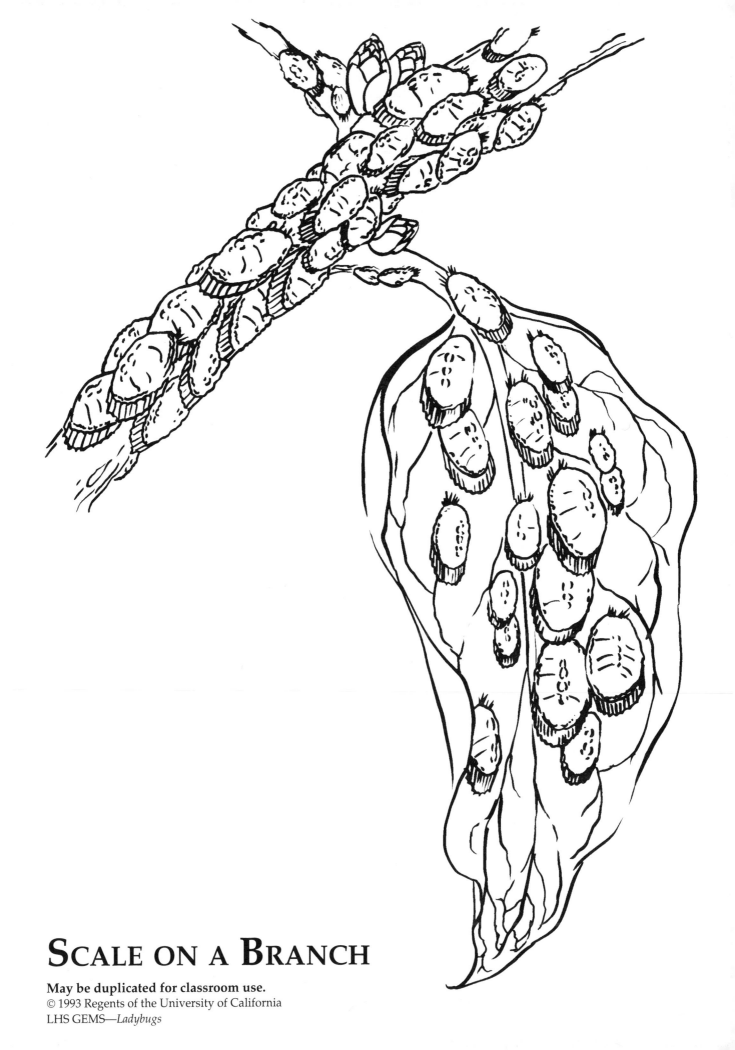

# SCALE ON A BRANCH

LADYBUG, EGGS, LARVAE, AND PUPA

**LADYBUG EATING APHIDS**

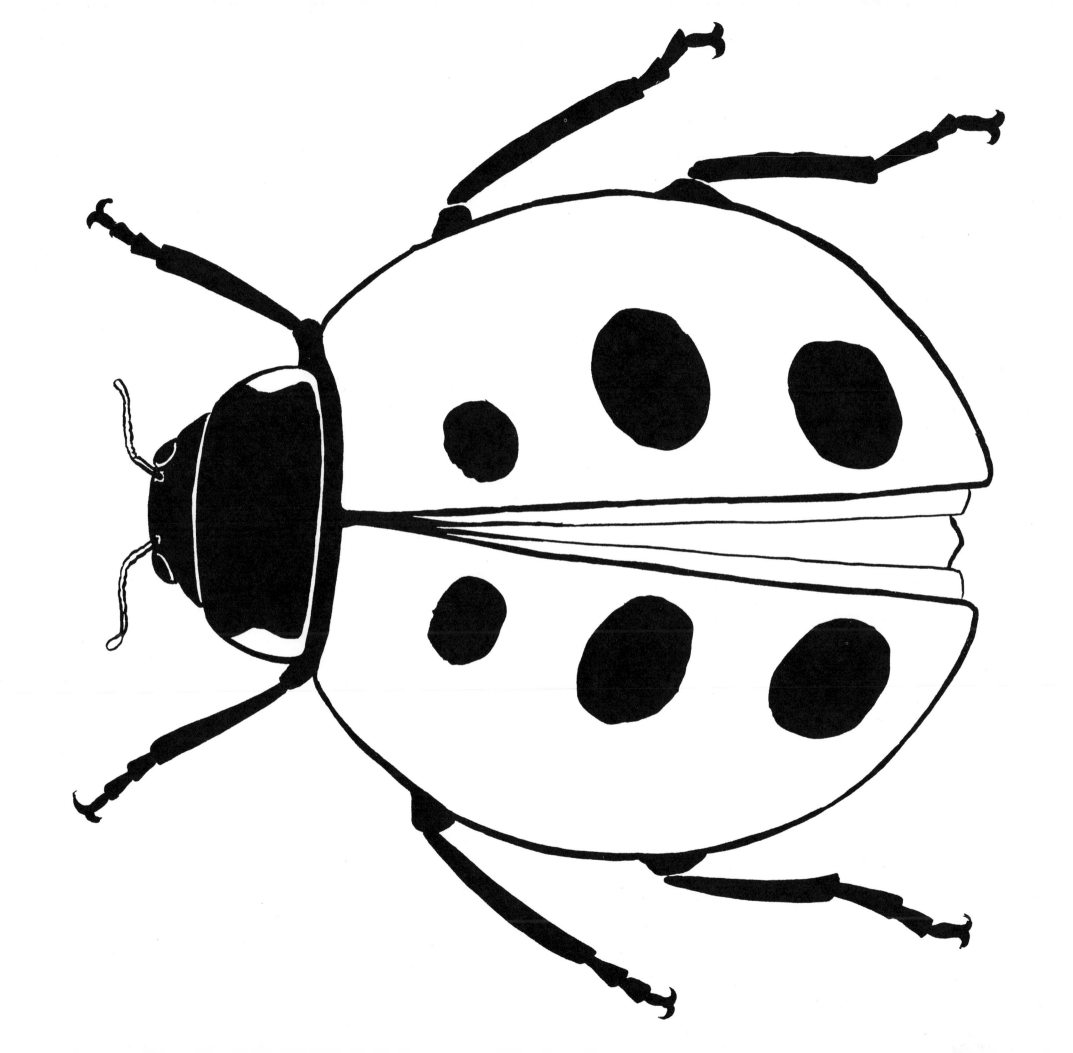

**LADYBUG**

# LADYBUG EGGS AND BABY LADYBUGS

# LARVAE AND PUPA